AS/A2 Sport Psychology Guide

Simon Webster

Jan Roscoe Publications

Published by Jan Roscoe Publications
Holyrood 23 Stockswell Road
Widnes
Cheshire WA8 4PJ
UK

tel - +44 (0)151 420 4446
fax - +44 (0)151 495 2622
E-mail - sales@jroscoe.co.uk
Internet - http://www.jroscoe.co.uk

Reprinted 2006, 2010

ISBN : 9781 901424 46 1

Cover photographs by Jan Roscoe.

Published via QuarkXpress 7
and Adobe Illustrator CS4

Printed and bound by Poplar Services Printers Ltd
Poplar House
Jackson Street
St Helens
WA9 3AP

tel - +44 (0)1744 23363
fax - +44 (0)1744 451242
E-mail - sales@poplarservices.com
Internet - http://www.poplarservices.com

INTRODUCTION

This book consists of a collection of notes and explanations suitable for background information for teachers of AS and A2 level Physical Education, or as student notes for those at the receiving end of the same courses.

At the time of going to press, there are three syllabuses available at AS and A2 levels :

AQA (Assessment and Qualifications Alliance) Sport and Physical Education. This is a modular syllabus incorporating Skill Acquisition and Sport Psychology (Module 1 - AS and Module 4 - A2).

OCR (Oxford, Cambridge and RSA Examinations) Physical Education. This modular syllabus includes Skill Acquisition as part of AS studies (Module 2562 section B), and Sport Psychology as an optional block of study in the A2 course (Module 2565 Option B2).

Edexcel Physical Education. Another modular syllabus in which the substantive part of Skill Acquisition is looked at in Unit 2 Section A (AS and A2), and Sport Psychology in Unit 6 Section B Option B, an optional feature of the A2 course.

This teacher resource fully supports the revised AS/A2 2008 AQA, OCR, Edexcel and WJEC syllabuses.

In each of the syllabuses, it will be expected that use and awareness of these elements of the courses should be reflected in the Personal or Individual Performance Portfolios of the students, and in the answers to Synoptic questions in the final exam.

The work from which the book has evolved has depended on about twelve years of A level teaching - thereby finding the best use of words and examples to illustrate points of theory.

Pages from the book are photocopy free within the purchasing institution, and should provide a complete and concise set of notes for the aspiring A level learner .

Dennis Roscoe (Editor)

CONTENTS

Section 1 Acquisition of Skill

CONTENTS

Section 2 Sport Psychology

CONTENTS

CONTENTS

Section 1 - Acquisition of Skill

Chapter 1 - SKILL AND ABILITY

Chapter 1 - SKILL AND ABILITY

THE CHARACTERISTICS OF SKILFUL PERFORMANCE

SKILL

Skill has been defined by Knapp (1977) as:

- The **learned ability** to bring about a predetermined result.
- Using the minimum of time or effort or both.

Skill is the capacity to make the **difficult seem easy**.

In order for a performance act to be classified as **skilful** it needs to be:

- **Learned**.
- **Efficient**.
- **Fluent**.
- **Aesthetic**.

- It must have an **end result** (for example, scoring a goal or winning a race).
- It must meet a set of **predetermined criteria** (for example, a gymnastic movement).

TYPES OF SKILL

A skill involving **movement** is known as a **Motor Skill**.

- A skill involving the interpretation of sensory information is known as a **Perceptual Motor Skill** (hitting, catching).
- Perceptual motor skills are often known as **Psychomotor Skills**.
- Most sporting skills are perceptual motor skills.
- They require the performer to **make decisions** based on information received by the senses (riding a bike, skiing, playing tennis).

- A skill requiring **thought** is known as a **Cognitive Skill**.

CLASSIFICATION OF MOVEMENT SKILLS

In order to learn more about a movement skill we need to separate out all the different aspects of that skill.
The separation should allow us to discover the **specific nature** of any one **skill**. We can then attempt to find methods to **improve** it.

For example, the javelin throw is:

- A complex skill, produced using large muscle groups.
- Requiring a large timing component.
- And can be repeated time and time again with little change.
- Consequently to train for javelin throwing the performer should try to develop power in large muscle groups.
- And should try to develop the timing element by practising the entire throw.

Chapter 1 - SKILL AND ABILITY

THE CLASSIFICATION CONTINUA

- Skills can be separated into **specific components**.
- A continuum is a **scale** ranging from high to low.
- A continuum is used to highlight **skills** with **varying levels** of any specific component.

THE MUSCULAR INVOLVEMENT CONTINUUM (GROSS-FINE SKILLS)

- **Gross motor skills** involve **large** muscle groups.
- **Fine motor skills** involve **small** muscle groups.

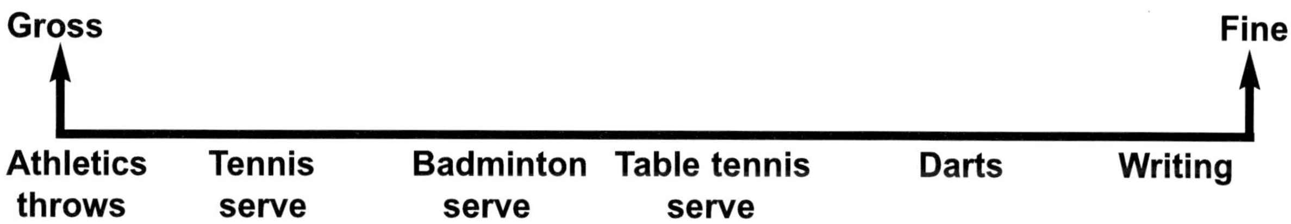

THE DIFFICULTY CONTINUUM (SIMPLE-COMPLEX SKILLS)

- **Simple skills** have a **small number** of parts.
- **Complex skills** have a **large number** of parts

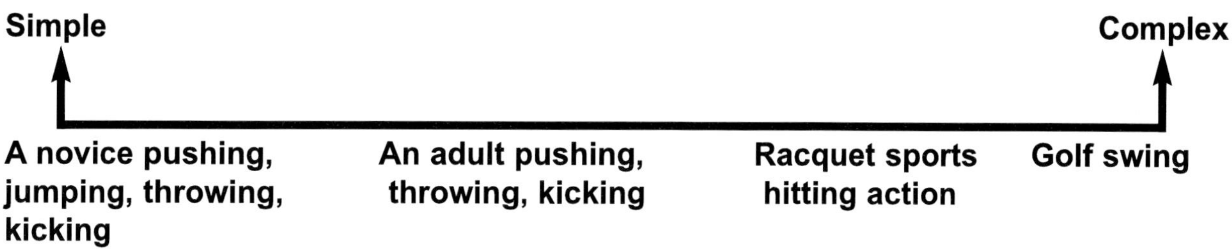

THE PACING CONTINUUM (SELF-PACED - EXTERNALLY-PACED SKILLS)

- For **Self-paced skills** the **timing** of the movement is determined by the **performer**.
- For **Externally-paced skills** the **timing** of the movement is affected / controlled by **external factors** (wind, weather, opponents).

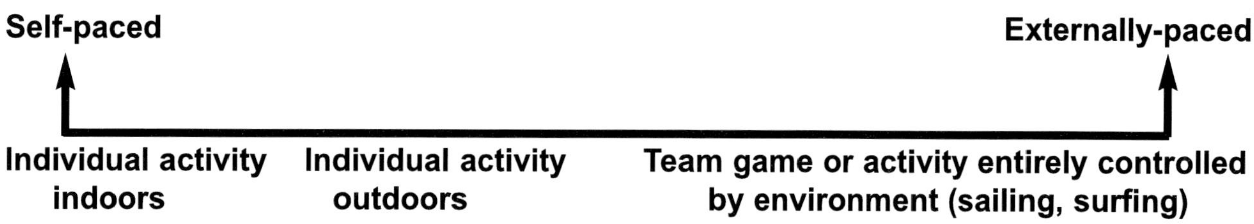

Chapter 1 - SKILL AND ABILITY

CONTINUITY (DISCRETE, CONTINUOUS AND SERIAL SKILLS)

- **Continuity** is a concept that **links** the number of **parts** of a skill to the time it takes to perform the skill.

Skill	Definition	Example
Discrete	A motor skill that has a clearly defined beginning and end point. Discrete skills are usually simple skills of very short duration.	Simple actions like a jump, hop, step, kick, punch, throw.
Continuous	A motor skill that has no clearly defined beginning or end point. The skill could therefore be of short, medium or long duration.	Running, swimming, cycling, rowing, walking.
Serial	A group of discrete skills joined together to make one complex skill or a sequence of skills.	Complex skills such as athletic throws and jumps. Sequences of skills like a gymnastic tumble or trampoline routine.

THE ORGANISATION CONTINUUM (HIGH-LOW SKILLS)

- Organisation refers to the **relationship** between the **parts** of the skill.
- The parts of a skill are known as **subroutines**.
- If the subroutines are **linked** in some way the skill is **highly organised**.
- If the subroutines are **not linked** the skill is said to be **low in organisation**.

For example, skills such as a tennis serve or golf drive are highly organised.
In order to correctly time a tennis serve or golf drive:

- The parts of the stroke need to occur at a particular time for a particular duration.
- The muscles used must contract with a particular amount of force.

Chapter 1 - SKILL AND ABILITY

THE ENVIRONMENTAL INFLUENCE CONTINUUM (OPEN-CLOSED SKILLS)

- **Closed Skills** are **not affected** by the **environment**; they are skills which are **self-paced**.
- **Open Skills** are **affected** by the environment; they are skills which are **externally-paced**.

Open ←————————————————→ **Closed**

Team games outdoors | **Team games indoors** | **Individual skill outdoors** | **Individual skill indoors**

Closed Skills	Open Skills
❐ **Closed skills** are those that can be **repeated** time and time again with little difference in the performance.	❐ **Open skills** are **difficult to repeat** because external factors cannot be controlled.
❐ **Closed skills** are **self-paced.**	❐ **Open skills** are **externally-paced**.
❐ **Closed skills** require the performer to concentrate on **kinaesthetic feedback** concerning the feelings connected with anatomical, mechanical, and physiological information from receptors within body systems.	❐ **Open skills** need the performer to **make decisions** concerning an ever changing environment.
❐ **Practising** for closed skills involves **repetitive practice** of set skills and routines.	❐ **Practising** for open skills involves **varied practice** of different skills in different situations.
	❐ When learning a **difficult open skill** it may be of benefit to **simplify** the skill. This can be achieved by making the skill more closed (**reduce external effects**). For example, reduce opposition, reduce the potential for variation.

Chapter 1 - SKILL AND ABILITY

DEFINITION AND CHARACTERISTICS OF ABILITY

The terms skill and ability often get confused. The table below outlines the major differences between the two.

Skill	Ability
❐ Skills are **learned**. ❐ Skills are **specific** qualities. ❐ Abilities are **needed** to **perform** skills. ❐ Skills can **vary over time** and can **change greatly** with practice. ❐ There are an **infinite number of** skills.	❐ Abilities are **inherited**. ❐ Abilities are **general** qualities. ❐ Abilities are generally **stable** over time but **can be improved**. ❐ It is difficult to predict the number of existing abilities. There are thought to be around **50 different abilities**.

MOTOR SKILL DEVELOPMENT

In order to be able to perform a **complex motor skill** a performer must first have been born with a number of **abilities**. At a young age the learner will **combine** a number of abilities in order to learn **simple skills** such as running, throwing, catching and jumping.

- These simple motor skills are known as **fundamental motor skills**. As the learner becomes more proficient he / she becomes able to adapt and refine the fundamental motor skills in order to perform **more complex skills** (increased number of parts).
  For example, a simple jump is refined to become the Fosbury flop, running becomes sprinting.

- Often it is assumed that performers are **natural all-round athletes**, that they have the ability to perform all sports. The concept of general motor ability assumes one overall ability.
  A person with good general motor ability would be able to perform a large number of skills well. There is **no definite evidence** for the existence of a **general motor ability**.

- Most researchers believe that **abilities** are **stable** and **enduring**. In other words they cannot change over time. However, some researchers believe that abilities **can be enhanced** at an early age through **practice** and increased access to facilities, equipment and coaching.

- The notion of **specific motor ability** assumes that different sports require **different motor abilities**. Each motor ability has **little direct relation** to any other motor ability. Just because a person is skilled in one activity it does not mean he / she will be skilled in all others. This concept is generally held as being true.

- **All-round athletes do exist**. They exist for a number of reasons including:
  - **Parental support** to develop excellence.
  - **Cultural pressure** for good sporting performance.
  - **Body size** (large strong performers could have an advantage at a number of sports).
  - **Personality traits** (a performer with a "sporting personality" would try hard and could do well at any sport).
  - **Coordination** (a person with a high element of coordination as a fitness component would learn skills more easily).

- **Simple skills** (for example, hitting and jumping) may involve **general motor abilities** and can therefore be transferred between activities.

Chapter 1 - SKILL AND ABILITY

TYPES OF ABILITY

Fleishman (1972) was one of the first to identify the existence of **different motor abilities**. He classified them under two headings:

- **Gross Motor Abilities**.
- **Perceptual Motor Abilities**.

A **gross motor ability** involves **large muscle groups** in the production of a movement.

Gross Motor Abilities	Examples of skills needing the Ability
❒ **Extent flexibility**	Static stretching, for example, a warm up or yoga session.
❒ **Dynamic flexibility**	Rapid ballistic stretching, for example, gymnastic tumbling.
❒ **Explosive strength**	Exerting a large force for a short period of time, for example, athletic throws.
❒ **Static strength**	A maximum exertion of force, for example, power lifting or tug of war.
❒ **Trunk strength**	Dynamic strength related to the abdominal area, for example, gymnastic pommel horse exercise.
❒ **Gross body equilibrium**	Maintaining balance without the benefit of sight, for example, somersault.
❒ **Gross body coordination**	Coordinating different body parts in order to make a movement, for example, a golf swing.
❒ **Stamina**	Continuing to exert a force over a period of time, for example, continuous swimming, cycling or rowing.
❒ **Limb speed**	Used when kicking or throwing.

A **perceptual motor ability** or psychomotor ability is an **innate capacity** of an individual to **interpret** and **use sensory information**. Major perceptual motor abilities include:

Perceptual Motor Ability	Examples of badminton skills needing the Ability
❒ **Coordination**	Overhead clear.
❒ **Speed**	Court coverage.
❒ **Reaction time**	Responding to opponent's smash.
❒ **Balance**	To achieve correct body position to play clear.
❒ **Agility**	Change direction quickly.
❒ **Arm hand steadiness**	Drop shot.
❒ **Aiming**	Short serve.
❒ **Depth perception**	Predicting position of shuttle in space.
❒ **Manual dexterity**	Changing from forehand to backhand grip.

Chapter 1 - SKILL AND ABILITY

Personal Performance Portfolio (Badminton)

1) Movement skills can be classified using a number of continua.
Classify:
a) a short badminton serve and
b) a jump smash during a game using the following continua:

- ❒ **gross - fine**
- ❒ **open - closed**
- ❒ **discrete - continuous - serial**
- ❒ **externally-paced - self-paced**
- ❒ **simple - complex**
- ❒ **high organisation - low organisation**.

In each case give reasons for your choice.

2) Name the gross motor abilities and psychomotor abilities which are most important during the performance of the following motor skills:
a) a jump smash
b) a short serve
c) recovery from overhead clear to return an opponent's drop shot by playing a low return.

In each case justify your answer.

Chapter 2 - INFORMATION PROCESSING DURING THE PERFORMANCE OF SKILLS IN PE

Chapter 2 - INFORMATION PROCESSING during the PERFORMANCE of SKILLS in PE

BASIC MODELS OF INFORMATION PROCESSING

An information processing model explains what happens if a performer decides to make a movement.

- A number of different models exist but they all share similar features. The simple model shown below outlines the main features of an information processing model.

A SIMPLE MODEL OF INFORMATION PROCESSING

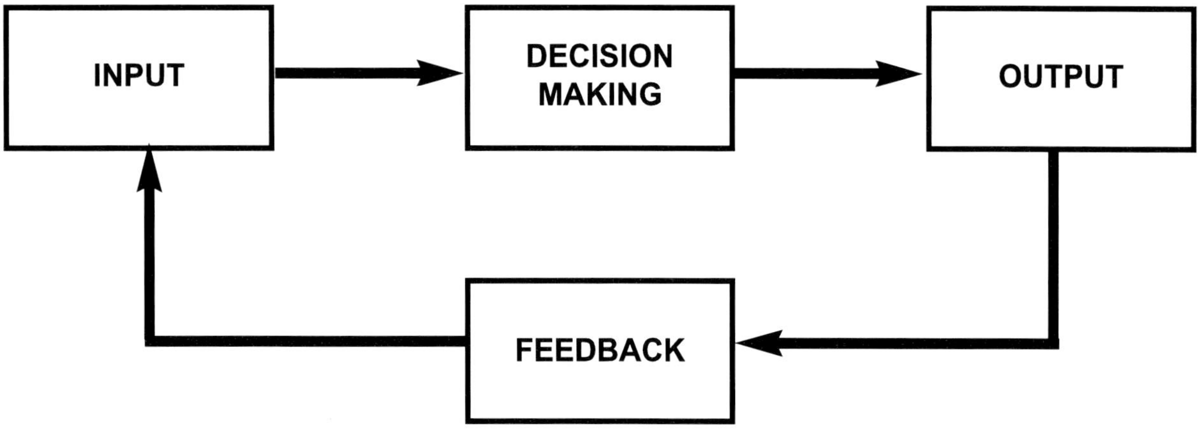

- **Input** is information entering the body from the senses.
- **Decision making** occurs in the brain.
- **Output** is the actual movement.
- **Feedback** is information concerning the movement.

For example, a cricket batter sees the cricket ball on a line to hit the stumps (**input**):

- The batter decides to play a defensive shot (**decision making**).
- The batter plays the defensive shot (**output**).
- The batter plays and misses and then hears the ball hit the stumps (**feedback**).

By learning more about **each stage** of the **information processing model**, performance at each stage can be **improved**.

For example, improved batting performance for the cricketer:

Stage of Model	Improved Performance by
❒ **Input**	Detecting the flight path of a cricket ball earlier and with greater accuracy.
❒ **Decision Making**	Realising that the ball will hit the stumps and selecting the appropriate shot.
❒ **Output**	Having the skill to play the chosen shot.
❒ **Feedback**	The batter sees the ball moving to the weaker hand of the fielder and decides to take a quick single.

Chapter 2 - INFORMATION PROCESSING during the PERFORMANCE of SKILLS in PE

WELFORD'S INFORMATION PROCESSING MODEL (1968)

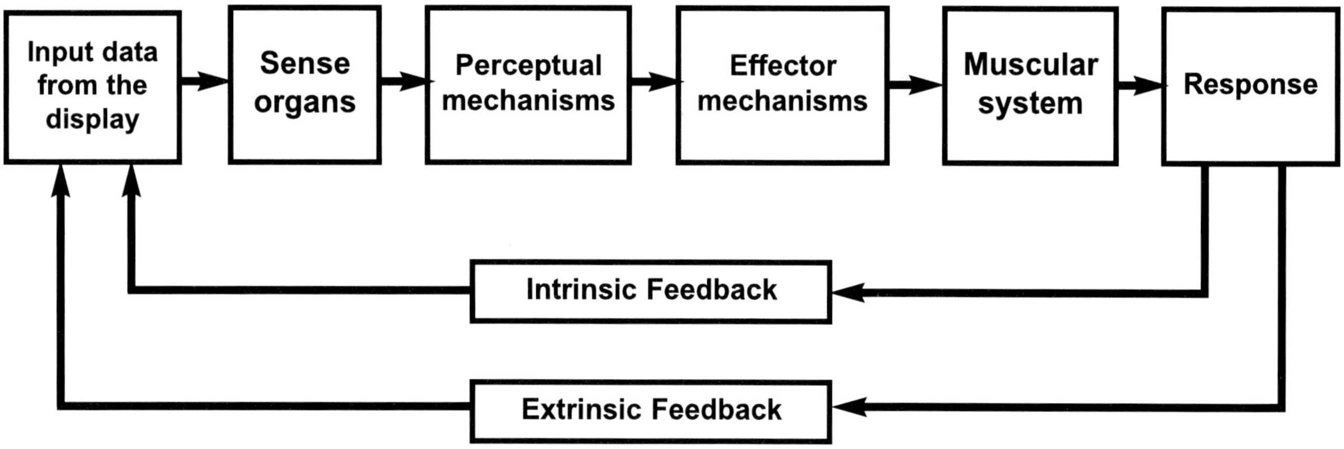

- **Input** is information entering the body from the senses. The **display** is the name given to the **environment**.
- The **sense organs** receive the information. In a sporting context, most information is received by the eyes, ears and muscles.
- **Perception** occurs in the brain. It is the process whereby the sensory input is given meaning. Perception involves the brain **comparing** present information with past information stored in the memory. Once the performer **understands** the input from the display he / she is able to make a decision concerning action.
- The **effector mechanisms** are the links between the brain and the muscles. Any decisions concerning movement are relayed to the muscles via nerves.
- The **muscular system** carries out the movement. The movement is termed **output**.
- **Intrinsic feedback** is information received by the **sense organs** through normal means.
- **Extrinsic feedback** is information given to the performer by an outside source.

Example of Welford's information processing model related to playing **Netball**:

Stage of Model	Action
❒ **Input**	The centre sees goal shooter get free of her marker. Goal attack is also free.
❒ **Perceptual Mechanism**	The centre perceives that goal attack is not ready to receive a pass. She perceives that goal shooter is ready to receive a pass. She uses memory to help her decide what to do, and decides to use a bounce pass to goal shooter.
❒ **Effector Mechanism**	The appropriate motor commands are sent to the muscles.
❒ **Output**	The pass is made by the muscular system.
❒ **Feedback**	The centre watches the successful execution of the pass.

Chapter 2 - INFORMATION PROCESSING during the PERFORMANCE of SKILLS in PE

WHITING'S INFORMATION PROCESSING MODEL

(adapted from Whiting, Acquiring Ball Skill, 1970)

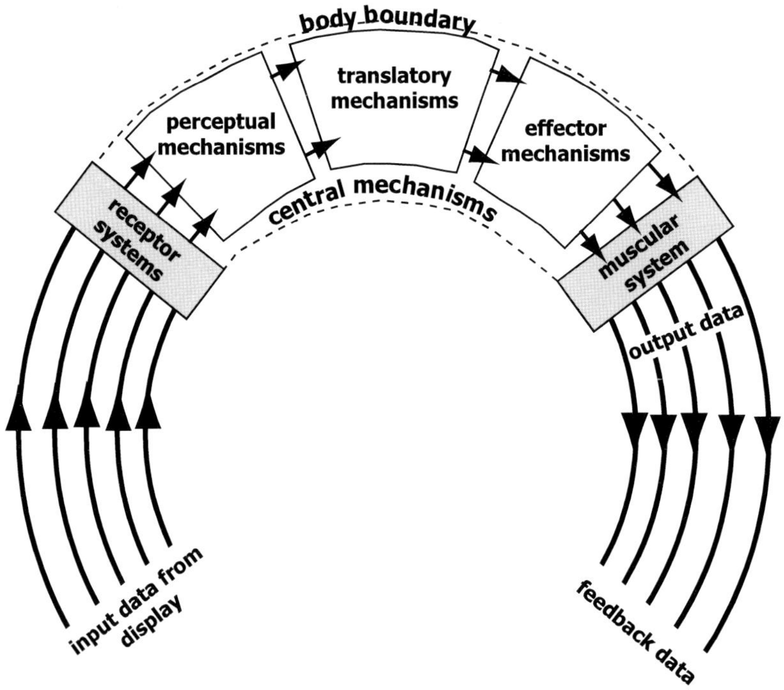

- **Input** is **information** entering the body from the senses via sensory neurones. The **display** is the name given to the **environment**.
- **Receptor systems** are the **sensory structures** (for example, eyes, touch, pain, smell, Golgi tendon organs which sense movement in tendons) which receive the information.
- **Perceptual Mechanisms** occur in the brain. They describe the process whereby the sensory input is given **meaning**. Perception involves the brain comparing present information with past information stored in the memory.
- In the model above, a number of arrows enter the perceptual mechanisms but only two arrows go to the translatory mechanisms. The reason for this is the fact that the brain can receive a large amount of information but can only process a **limited** amount of information. This concept is known as **limited attentional capacity**.
- The **Translatory Mechanism** is the part of the brain in which decisions are made. Translation refers to the process whereby information from the perceptual mechanisms is used to help form a **motor programme** or plan of action, which can then be sent to the effector mechanisms.
- The **Effector Mechanisms** are the links between the brain and the muscles. Any decisions concerning movement are relayed to the voluntary muscles via efferent neurones (nerves).
- The **muscular system** carries out the movement. This movement is termed **output**.

Chapter 2 - INFORMATION PROCESSING during the PERFORMANCE of SKILLS in PE

SCHMIDT'S INFORMATION PROCESSING MODEL (1975)

- **Stimulus Identification** refers to the reception and interpretation of sensory information (input and perception).
- **Response Selection** is responsible for decision making.
- **Response Programming** is concerned with the sending of movement information via the efferent neurones (nerves) to voluntary muscles.
- **Output** is movement.

Example of Schmidt's Information processing model related to a rugby fly half receiving possession from the scrum half:

Stage of Model	Example
❒ **Stimulus Identification**	Fly half identifies the position of ball in space, the direction and speed of pass, the position of team mates and the position of opposition.
❒ **Response Selection**	Fly half decides whether to run, pass or kick.
❒ **Response Programming**	Fly half decides to kick and sends a motor programme to voluntary muscles to carry out the skill.
❒ **Output**	Fly half kicks to touch.

Chapter 2 - INFORMATION PROCESSING during the PERFORMANCE of SKILLS in PE

THE INFORMATION PROCESSING MODEL

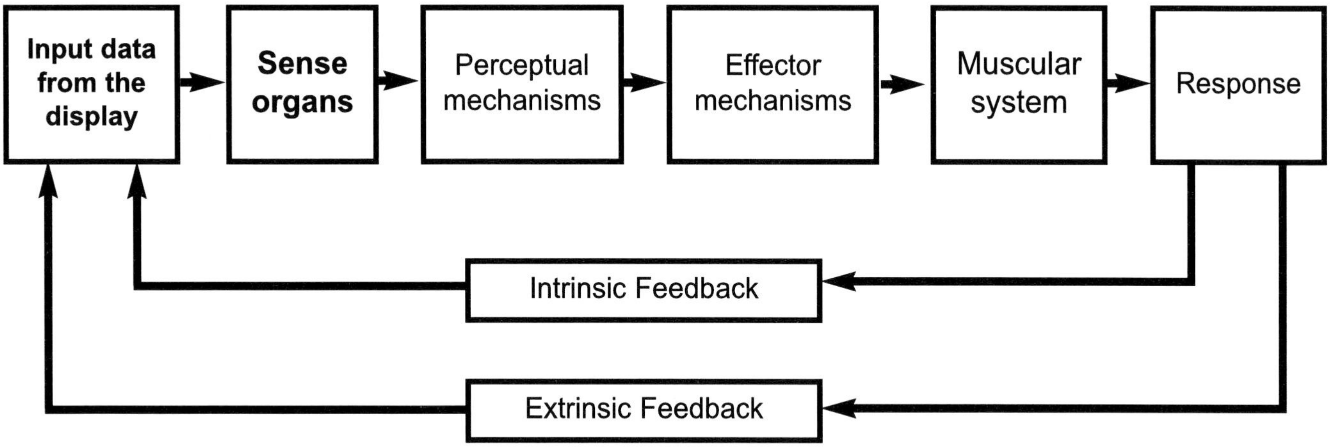

SENSORY INPUT AND ATTENTION

The following pages refer to the first two elements of the information processing model.

Chapter 2 - INFORMATION PROCESSING during the PERFORMANCE of SKILLS in PE

SENSORY INPUT AND ATTENTION

Sensory input is **information received** through the senses via sensory neurones:

- **Sight (vision)**.
- **Sound (audition)**.
- **Feel (kinaesthesis)**.
- **Smell (olfaction)**.
- **Taste**.

- The three most important forms of sensory information for the performer are **vision**, **kinaesthesis** and **audition**.
- Sensory information provides all performers with a **knowledge of performance** and **knowledge of results** which function to motivate, reinforce and direct behaviour.
- The experienced performer will show an ability to **concentrate** on the most important sensory information.
- The process by which the performer concentrates on sensory information is known as **attention**.

ATTENTION

The amount of information we can attend to is limited. We have **limited attentional capacity**. Too much sensory information can **overload** the performer.

- Because of **limited attentional capacity** it is important that the performer attends to the **relevant cues** (important information) and rejects the irrelevant cues (unimportant information). This is known as **selective attention**.
  For example, a teacher can **alter** the visual display of a pupil to make it easier to selectively attend:
  - A two-tone cricket ball makes spin easier to identify.
  - A newly painted hockey ball stands out more on a pitch.

- The use of **simulators** and **training machines** provides the opportunity to safely practise selective attention. Often they are used to enable safer practice and speed up learning by controlling environmental factors. The **practice environment** can be **controlled** to help the learner to perceive his / her sensory information more effectively and quicker. For example:
  - Windsurfer trainers.
  - Cricket catching cradles.
  - Scrummaging machines.
  - Golf simulators.

- When we reach the **autonomous stage of learning**, some parts of **performance** become **automatic**. As a consequence we do not need to attend to those parts. This gives the performer **spare attentional capacity**. Spare attentional capacity will allow the performer to attend to **new elements of a skill** such as tactics or anticipating the moves of an opponent. Hence the teacher needs to get the **performer** to the **autonomous stage of learning**.

- The teacher will also need to help the performer to concentrate, to **focus** the **attention** of the performer and to **reduce** the chance of **attentional switching** to unimportant information. One way to avoid attentional switching is to make activity **interesting**.

- According to **Hawthorne**, performance changes for the better when **changes** are made to the **learning or performing environment**, and pupils get bored if the teacher uses the same drills.

Chapter 2 - INFORMATION PROCESSING during the PERFORMANCE of SKILLS in PE

THE SINGLE CHANNEL THEORY (Broadbent 1958)

The theories of information processing attempt to answer the questions: How much information can we attend to? Can we attend to more than one thing at a time?

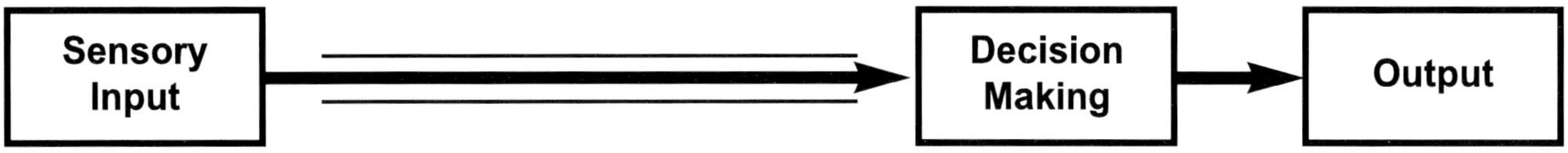

- The **single channel theory** says that we can only attend to **one thing at a time**.
- Information gets processed **sequentially**, one at a time, one after the other.
- Some theorists believe there is some form of **attentional switching** that allows the performer to monitor and react to different informational stimuli. This gives the impression of being able to attend to two things at once. In reality it's still only one thing at a time, for example, the cocktail party effect.
- Theorists suggest the only way two things can be attended to at the same time is if they require a **small amount of attentional capacity**. Two pieces of simple information are small enough to pass along the single channel.

THE MULTIPLE CHANNEL THEORY (Kahneman 1973)

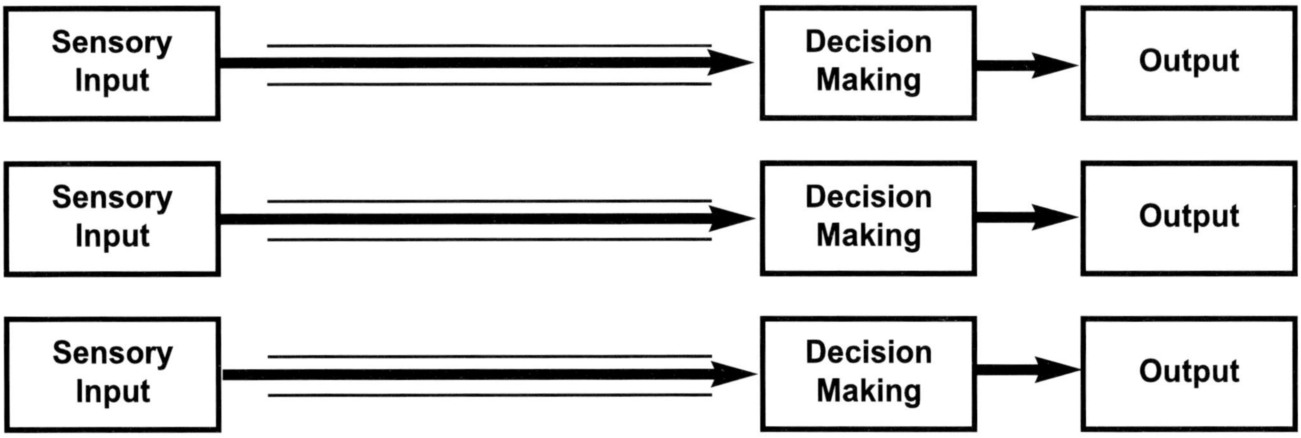

- The **multiple channel theory** says that so long as the incoming information comes along **different channels** the performer could complete **more than one task**.
- An advanced games player will not need to attend to a large amount of information because certain **actions are automatic**. **Spare attentional capacity** can be used to attend to more than one task.
- **Effort** is perceived as taking up **attentional capacity**.
- A **skilled player** will be able to attend to a second task as the amount of **effort** expended on the first task could be **minimal**.

Chapter 2 - INFORMATION PROCESSING during the PERFORMANCE of SKILLS in PE

TEACHING FOR ATTENTION

The brain can only attend to a limited amount of information. It is important that the performer attends to the relevant information and disregards irrelevant information. This process is known as **selective attention**. Attention and selective attention can be improved in a number of ways.

Reduce the attentional demands during skill learning

- Skills are often learnt **more quickly** if they are broken down into **parts**.
  This enables the learner to **fully concentrate** on the **most important parts** of the skill and prevents the learner from becoming overloaded with information and so confused.
  For example, the lay-up in basketball can be broken down into:
  - The running dribble.
  - The one-two step.
  - The jump and release.

Ensure basic skills are learned to the autonomous stage before progressing to more advanced skills.

- If the learner can **automatically** produce the first or **easy parts** of a skill, this will "free-up" **spare attentional capacity** which can be used to solve **more difficult skill** problems.
- Often learners are stuck on so-called **learning plateaux** and are unable to move on because they do **not** have the attentional capacity which will enable them to make further progress.

Do not overload the learner with information

- **Too many cues** from the teacher or environment will **overload** the learner.
  The teacher needs to reduce the cues by controlling the environment.
  For example:
  - Learning in **semi-opposed** rather than fully-opposed situations.
  - Teaching instructions kept to a **minimum**.
- The teacher must also **highlight the cues** that are important, suggesting to the learner what they should be attending to.

Do not underload the learner

- **Too little information** will underload the system leading to **inattentiveness** and **loss of motivation**.

Chapter 2 - INFORMATION PROCESSING during the PERFORMANCE of SKILLS in PE

TEACHING FOR ATTENTION (continued)

Selective attention and stage of learning

- During the **early** stages of learning, **visual information** is most important. Consequently, the teacher should instruct the learner to attend to the **most important** visual cues.

- Later, **kinaesthetic information** becomes more **important**.
  Consequently, the teacher should instruct the learner to attend to **how the movement felt**.

Improve concentration

- Pupils must learn how to **concentrate** on the relevant cues and **disregard** the **irrelevant cues** if they are to fully use their attentional capacity.

- The teacher must retain learners' interest by **introducing new tasks**, and by making existing tasks **more challenging**.

- **Positive reinforcement** should be used when correct performance is observed. **Negative reinforcement** and **punishment** should also be used when appropriate to ensure **maximum concentration**.

The effects of arousal levels on attentional capacity

- **Arousal** levels have an effect on **attentional capacity**. Too much arousal can **reduce** attentional capacity. This is sometimes termed **narrowing of the attentional field** and can be likened to a games player wearing blinkers.
  This is detrimental to some sports where players need to be **aware** of everything going on around them.
  For example, a quarterback in American Football.

- Conversely, for sports that have **small attentional demands** it is a bonus to be able to shut out unwanted interference.
  For example, weight lifting.

- **Too little arousal** can also **reduce** attentional capacity.

- It is important for the teacher or coach to make certain that his / her athletes perform with the appropriate level of arousal for their activity.

Chapter 2 - INFORMATION PROCESSING during the PERFORMANCE of SKILLS in PE

THE INFORMATION PROCESSING MODEL

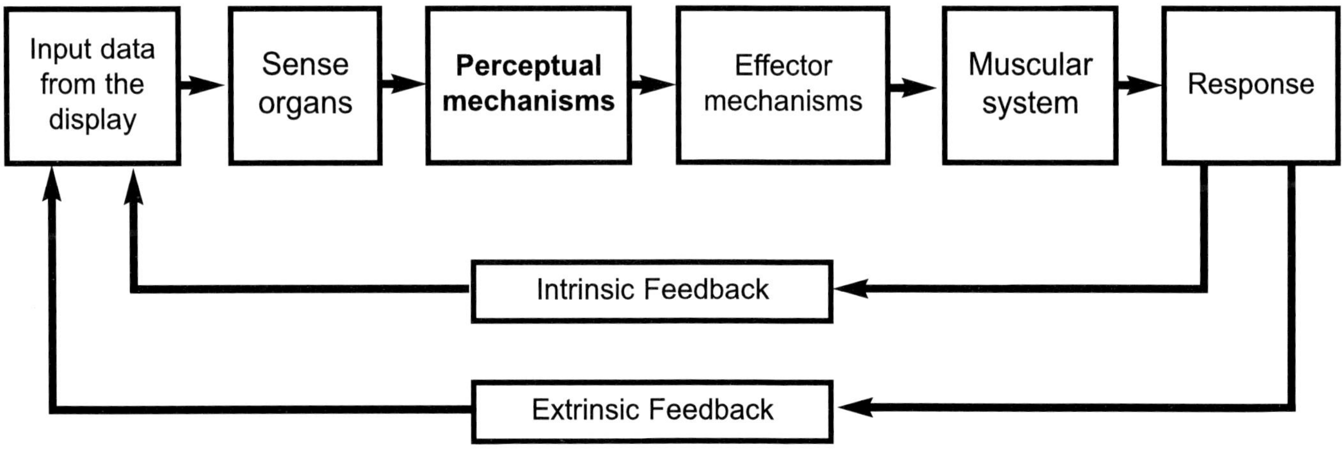

PERCEPTUAL MECHANISMS (MEMORY)

The following pages refer to this next element of the information processing model.

Chapter 2 - INFORMATION PROCESSING during the PERFORMANCE of SKILLS in PE

MEMORY

"The capacity that permits organisms to benefit from their past experiences."

The 3 types of memory:

- **Short-term sensory store**.
- **Short-term memory**.
- **Long-term memory**.

SHORT-TERM SENSORY STORE (STSS)

- **All information** from the senses is passed through the STSS.
- Information is kept for **up to 1 second**.
- If the information is not considered important **it is lost and forgotten** and replaced by new information.

SHORT-TERM MEMORY (STM) OR WORKING MEMORY

The functions of the short-term memory are:

- To **receive information** from the short-term sensory store and long-term memory.
- To **send information** to the **long-term memory**.
- To aid in **decision making**.
- Information **not considered important** is forgotten.

The 3 major characteristics are:

Duration:

- The amount of **time new information is kept** before being lost.
- It lasts between 20-30 seconds before we lose the information.
  For example, a new telephone number.

Capacity:

- **How much information** we can **remember**.
- As a rule, 7 items, + or - 2 items.
- This can be improved by "**chunking**" information, placing it into **easily remembered** groups.
  For example, 768594032 becomes 768 594 032.

Processing:

- **How the information is used.**
  For example, it can be used to solve a problem or to accomplish a task.
  Or it can be stored in the long-term memory for future use.

Chapter 2 - INFORMATION PROCESSING during the PERFORMANCE of SKILLS in PE

LONG-TERM MEMORY (LTM)

- Long-term memory is a very **well-learned store** of **past experiences**.
- LTM is **limitless**, and once in LTM **information is not forgotten**.
- Although information may be stored in the LTM, this does **not mean** that it is **easily recalled**.
- Information is **coded** and the performer must be able to **connect** the **memory** to the **code** before he / she can **recall** the memory.

The three main parts of LTM are:

PROCEDURAL MEMORY

- This is information about **how** to do something.
- The **correct procedure** or order.
- The procedural memory serves as a "**blueprint**" when you need to **repeat** a movement, a sort of **recall schema**.

SEMANTIC MEMORY

- This is a **knowledge** memory.
- General **facts** and **concepts** are stored here.
- If the procedural memory is the "**how**" the semantic memory is the "**what**".
  For example, knowledge of football trivia or concepts such as the sweeper system and offside trap.

EPISODIC MEMORY

- This is knowledge about **personally experienced events**.
  For example, your first kiss.

THE RELATIONSHIP BETWEEN STSS, STM and LTM (Schmidt 1990)

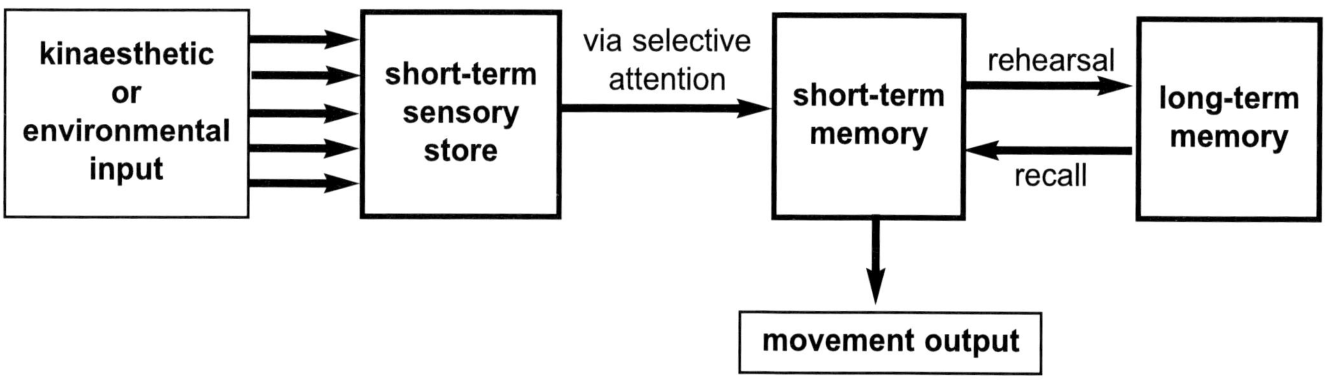

- **Large amounts** of sensory information **pass** through the **short-term sensory store**.
- The information is **filtered** through the process of **selective attention** before being passed onto the **short-term memory**.
- Information in the short-term memory can be used to help **decide** on a **movement** outcome.
- Alternatively, **well-rehearsed** information can be passed onto the **long-term memory**.
- In order to decide upon a correct course of action, information from the short-term memory can be combined with information **recalled** from the long-term memory.

Chapter 2 - INFORMATION PROCESSING during the PERFORMANCE of SKILLS in PE

MEMORY AND PERFORMANCE

The following example is used to show how a **goalkeeper** uses both **STM** and **LTM** to help save a penalty:

- The keeper uses information from the STM to **assess** the opponents' actions. For example, the way the player runs towards the ball, the angle the kicking foot makes with the ball.
- The keeper compares **present information** from STM with **past experience** (LTM) before deciding what to do.
- **Episodic memory** provides examples of what this player and other players have done **in the past**.
- **Semantic memory** provides information on **what the keeper should do** in this **situation**.
- **Procedural memory** provides information on **how to perform** the selected skill.

HOW TO IMPROVE MEMORY, A COACHES GUIDE

To improve memory, information needs to be transferred from STSS to STM to LTM as quickly as possible. How?

- **Instructions** need to be **clear** and **concise**. Too much information and the performer will forget.
- Provide **lots of practice**. Well-learned tasks are more easily transferred to LTM. Skills must therefore be overlearned.
- **Speed of learning**. Things that are learned quickly are more likely to be forgotten.
- **Information** is most easily remembered in **picture form**, so try to use examples that enable the performer to picture the correct technique / tactic.
  For example, "**the toilet position**" gives a mental picture of the body position needed when setting up a rugby maul.
- Use phrases and sayings which can be **easily remembered**.
  For example, "**chin-knee-toe**", when describing the alignment of body parts during the preparation phase of the shot putt.
- The **Von Restorf** effect. Any information that is presented in a **novel way** will be remembered. Make a performance out of teaching, make it **different** and **interesting**.

Chapter 2 - INFORMATION PROCESSING during the PERFORMANCE of SKILLS in PE

THE INFORMATION PROCESSING MODEL

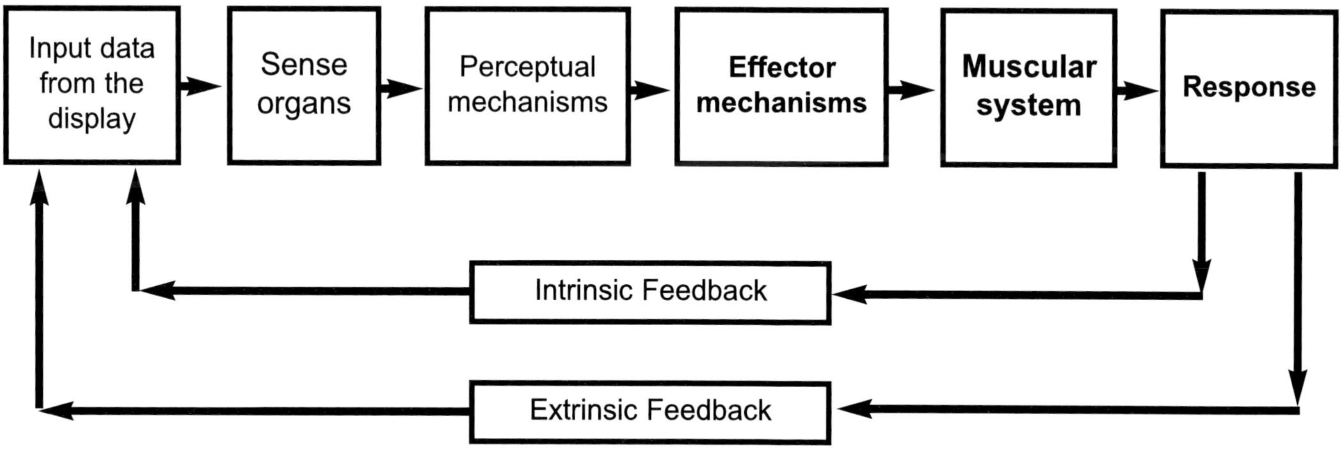

EFFECTOR AND MUSCULAR SYSTEMS

(REACTION TIME AND ANTICIPATION)

The following pages refer to the next three elements of the information processing model.

Chapter 2 - INFORMATION PROCESSING during the PERFORMANCE of SKILLS in PE

REACTION TIME

The coach needs to improve the performer's decision making processes. Improvements in reaction time and the ability to anticipate the moves of an opponent will help the performer make decisions more quickly and more effectively.

RESPONSE TIME = REACTION TIME + MOVEMENT TIME

- **Response time** is the time taken to **react** to a stimulus and respond through movement.
  For example, the response time for a sprint start would be the time difference between the gun going off and the athlete's rear foot leaving the block.

- **Reaction time** is the amount of time **between** a **stimulus** and the **first movement** initiated in response to the stimulus.
  For example, the reaction time at the start of a sprint race would be the time between the gun going off and the start of pressure being applied to the starting blocks.

TYPES OF REACTION TIME

- **Simple reaction time**:
  - **One stimulus** and one response.
    For example, response to the starter's gun.

- **Choice reaction time**:
  - Only **one response** must be made to **several stimuli**.
  - The correct stimulus must be chosen and then responded to.
    For example, a bowler could bowl different line and length. The batter must identify the line and length before selecting a shot.

- The **more choices** a person has, the **more information needs processing**, the **longer it takes** to process the information, the **slower the reaction time**.

- **Movement time**:
  - This is the time taken for a movement or action to be completed **once the movement has been initiated**.
    For example, the movement time during a sprint start would be the time taken from the start of pressure being applied to the blocks until the athlete's rear foot leaves the blocks.

Chapter 2 - INFORMATION PROCESSING during the PERFORMANCE of SKILLS in PE

HICK'S LAW

According to Hick (1952), **increasing the number of stimuli** (each of which the performer then has to process) **increases a performer's reaction time**:

- After a certain point an **increase** in the number of alternative stimuli brings about **no change** in reaction time.
- The reason for this is because the performer has **limited attentional capacity**.
- The performer can become easily **overloaded** with a large number of stimuli to process.
- Adding **more** information (which would then need to be processed) would **make no difference** to a performer who is already overloaded.

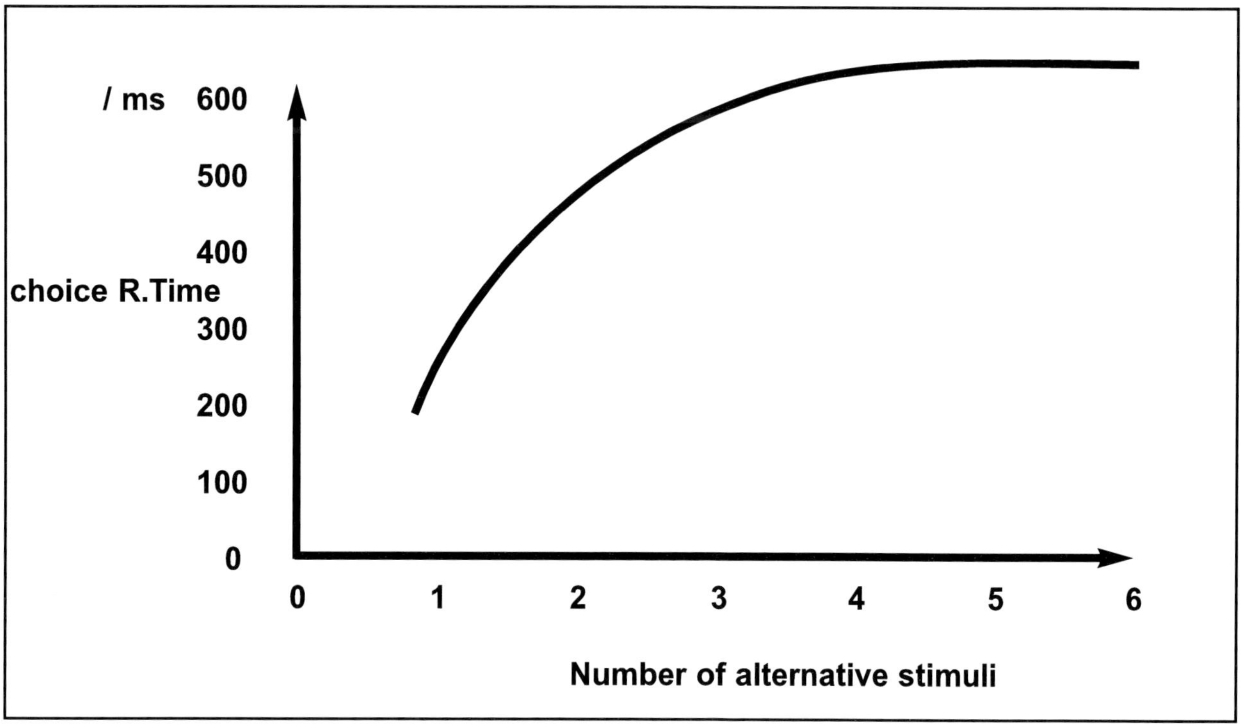

- Simple reaction time may be about **200ms** (milliseconds) - or slightly less for top class speed athletes.
- The cut off point below which a sprint start is deemed a false start is 100ms.
- When the alternatives are **increased to two** the reaction time nearly **doubles**.
- Hence Hick's Law is significant for sports players.
- A player should always try to **keep his / her opponent guessing** in an attempt to slow the opponent's reaction time. Vary play and do not be predictable.

Chapter 2 - INFORMATION PROCESSING during the PERFORMANCE of SKILLS in PE

THE PSYCHOLOGICAL REFRACTORY PERIOD (PRP)

❐ The **PRP** is the label for the theory explaining why a performer is unable to quickly respond to a **dummy** or fake move. The **PRP** is the **time taken to react to a second stimulus** after a first stimulus has occurred.

❐ It refers to the **time taken to react** once an individual has realised that he / she **has responded in an incorrect way** and **wants to change** the response.
For example, you react to an opponent's tennis shot by shaping to play a forehand, then you realise you should be playing a backhand.

❐ In other words, the **PRP** is the **time taken to change your mind**. In sport the PRP is generally the time it takes to respond to an opponent's fake or dummy.

❐ It happens because the brain has a **limited ability** to **process information**. We have difficulty in dealing with more than one stimulus at a time, so we deal with the first stimulus before moving onto a second stimulus.

❐ Our eyes may **tell us** that we have been faked but we **cannot do anything about it** until the **brain** has finished processing the initial response.
For example, a rugby player throws a dummy, the defender responds thinking that a pass is being made. The defender is unable to attempt to tackle the attacker until the motor programme for responding to a pass is finished.

❐ The PRP can be as much as **0.5 seconds**, so it is **very important** to use **fakes** and **dummies** in order to **slow down the reactions** of an opponent.

Chapter 2 - INFORMATION PROCESSING during the PERFORMANCE of SKILLS in PE

ANTICIPATION

- Anticipation has been defined as the **ability** to **predict future events** from early signals or past events.
  For example, a goal keeper dives to save a penalty before the ball has been struck.

- Quick reaction times are often the difference between success and failure. Reaction time can be **speeded up** if the performer learns to **anticipate** certain actions. Good performers **start** running **motor programmes before** the stimulus is fully recognised. In other words they anticipate the strength, speed and direction of a stimulus.

- Remember that your **opponent** will also be trying to anticipate. Reactions can be slowed by:
  - Varying play.
  - Using fakes and dummies.
  - Trying to increase choice reaction time.

FACTORS AFFECTING RESPONSE TIME AND METHODS TO REDUCE REACTION TIME

- Reaction time increases with **age**, with reaction times for **females** increasing less than those of males. In addition, **males** have quicker reactions than **females**. Consequently when playing a person with slower reactions, give him / her **less time to process information**.
  For example, a racquet sports player should play at a high tempo, hitting the ball hard and imparting a great deal of speed onto the ball.

- Reaction time is improved as **stimulus intensity** increases. Teachers should highlight **relevant cues**.
  For example, the use of two colour cricket balls to highlight spin.

- Conversely, performers should **disguise play** to increase opponents' reaction time.
  For example, cricket bowlers try to hide the shiny side of the ball from the batter to prevent the batter from guessing which way the ball may swing.

- **Tall people** are more likely to have slower reactions than shorter people because of the increased distance information has to travel from the brain to the working muscles. This partly explains why short sprinters tend to be good starters in the 60m sprint.

- **Arousal** levels affect reaction time. Reaction times are **quickest** when the performer is **alert but not over excited**. Coaches often try to keep athletes calm during stressful situations. Often successful sprinters look focused yet calm, whilst other athletes seem agitated.

- **Selectively attend** to the opponents' most **important cues**. This will give the performer clues about how to anticipate.
  For example, the position of an opponent's body, or the direction he / she is looking. The coach should identify which cues to attend to.

- **Predict** an opponent's play by identifying consistencies in his / her play.
  For example, an opponent's favourite move or shot. An **opponent** may be using a **fake** or dummy every other stroke.

- **Be prepared**, think for all eventualities.

Chapter 2 - INFORMATION PROCESSING during the PERFORMANCE of SKILLS in PE

THE INFORMATION PROCESSING MODEL

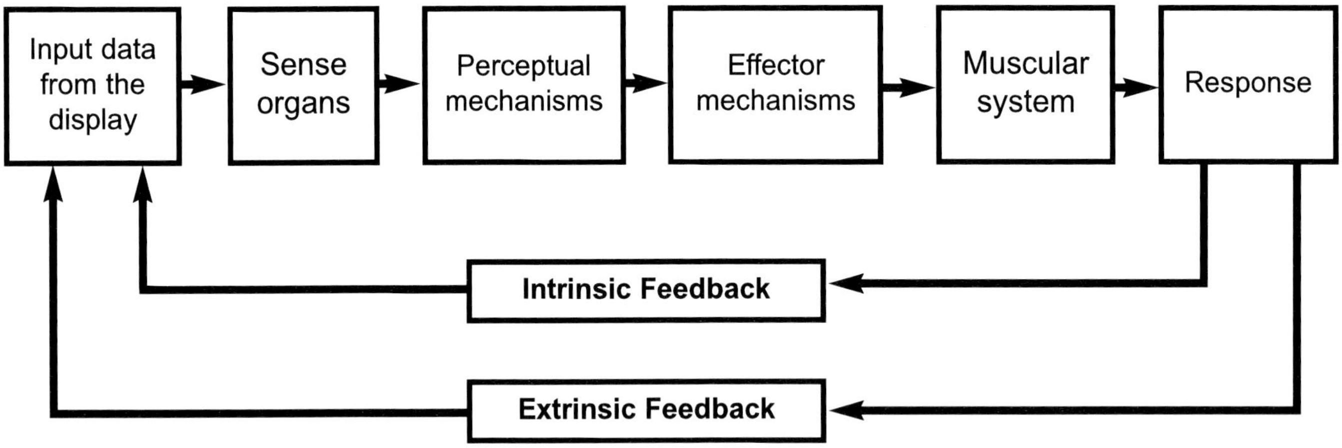

FEEDBACK

The following pages refer to the feedback elements of the information processing model.

Chapter 2 - INFORMATION PROCESSING during the PERFORMANCE of SKILLS in PE

FEEDBACK

Feedback has been defined as **any** kind of **sensory information**, not just that concerning errors.

TYPES OF FEEDBACK

INTRINSIC FEEDBACK

- According to Schmidt, **intrinsic** feedback is **sensory information** that normally occurs when individuals produce **movement**.
- **Intrinsic** feedback received from **outside** the body (via surface receptors such as touch, pressure, pain and skin temperature) is known as **exteroceptive** feedback.
- **Intrinsic** feedback from **within** the body is known as **proprioceptive / kinaesthetic** feedback. Proprioceptors are the internal sensory receptors (interoceptors) such as the vestibular apparatus which is concerned with balance, and Golgi tendons and muscle spindles which are concerned with joint angles and muscle forces.

EXTRINSIC FEEDBACK

- According to Schmidt, **extrinsic** feedback is **sensory information provided by a source**, and is additional to that which occurs normally.

For a 100m race:

INTRINSIC	EXTRINSIC
❐ **Sight**: seeing other runners. ❐ **Sound**: hearing opposition / crowd. ❐ **Proprioception**: position of limbs and body in space, and muscle tension, needed for smooth coordinated movement. ❐ **Smell**.	❐ **Knowledge of performance**: information about **performance**. Technical information from a number of sources including the coach, information from video, film, newspaper. ❐ **Knowledge of results**: information concerning the **outcome**. For example, success or failure, distance / time. Information can be from a number of sources: ❐ Coach. ❐ Video. ❐ Newspapers. ❐ Others.

CONCURRENT FEEDBACK

- **Concurrent Feedback** occurs during a movement.

TERMINAL FEEDBACK

- **Terminal Feedback** occurs post-performance.

Chapter 2 - INFORMATION PROCESSING during the PERFORMANCE of SKILLS in PE

FUNCTIONS OF EXTRINSIC FEEDBACK

MOTIVATION

- Information concerning **success** and **failure** can be **motivational**.
  - Success is motivational.
  - Failure can act as a spur to motivate.

REINFORCEMENT

- According to **Thorndike's Law of Effect**, **behaviour** that is **rewarded** will tend to be **repeated**.
- **Positive** and **negative reinforcement** will increase the chance of the performer repeating the performance.
  For example, if the performer is **praised** after correct performance, the performer is liable to want to **repeat** the performance.

INFORMATION

- **Extrinsic feedback provides information** about **errors** and therefore provides the basis for error correction.

PROBLEMS

- Performers can become **dependent** on extrinsic feedback. When **feedback is withdrawn** performance can **deteriorate**.
- The performer repeats a performance in order to receive extrinsic feedback.
  Hence once feedback is withheld there becomes no reason to repeat the performance.
- The **coach** should gradually **phase out extrinsic feedback** in order to reduce the effects of feedback dependency.

QUALITIES OF EFFECTIVE FEEDBACK

- **Visual feedback** for the beginner should be used to help the performer gain a mental picture of the performance. During **later stages of learning**, visual feedback should be used to highlight specific elements of the skill which need attention.
- Any **demonstrations** used should be totally **correct**. Remember that the performer will be trying to **copy** the demonstration.
- **Verbal feedback** should be **specific** and **precise**. **Too much** information at the **early stage** of learning can **overload** the performer. At the **later stages** of learning the performer should have **spare attentional capacity**. This will enable him / her to attend to more detailed and lengthy bouts of verbal feedback.
- **Verbal feedback** should help the performer make **better use** of his / her own **intrinsic feedback (kinaesthesis)**. The coach should ask the novice questions related to how the movement felt. Verbal feedback relating to future **targets** should be **challenging** yet **attainable**.
- **Positive feedback** is more **effective** than negative feedback.

Chapter 3 - MOTOR CONTROL OF SKILLS IN PHYSICAL EDUCATION

Chapter 3 - MOTOR CONTROL OF SKILLS IN PHYSICAL EDUCATION

MOTOR AND EXECUTIVE PROGRAMMES

- The theories behind **executive programmes** and **subroutines** explain how motor skills are performed. They also explain how a performer is able to move from learning **simple** skills **to** performing **complex** sequences of movements.

- The **executive programme** is a **store** of information; it contains all the information necessary to make a movement. When a performer decides to make a movement it calls up a **motor programme** from the **long-term memory**.

- **Subroutines** are the **parts** that make up the **executive programme**.

- Subroutines are fixed and run off **automatically**. They can be changed if the **executive programme** is **changed**.

- **Executive programmes** decide the order of the subroutines. They make decisions and are flexible.

- The **novice's** subroutines are liable to be **less specific** than those of a **skilled performer** and (consequentially) will probably be inappropriate or ineffective.

Learning takes place when the performer is able to transform simple skills into more complex skills by **increasing the number of parts of the skill**. **Motor programme theory** states that the performer is able to do this by transforming existing executive programmes into subroutines of a new more complex executive programme. The **new executive programme** contains **more information** and more complex subroutines.

- This is achieved in the following way:
  - As the subroutines become **learned**, more and more subroutines become **automatic**.
  - This gives the performer **spare attentional capacity** which can be used to concentrate on new information.
  - New information can be added to previous executive programmes.
  - In this way old executive programmes can become subroutines of a new and more complex executive programme.

  For example, when playing tennis, the novice's initial motor programme is likely to be one for simply hitting the ball.
    - The motor programme would be very simple and have very few subroutines.
    - Through practice and the development of spare attentional capacity, the motor programme can be changed from hitting the ball to producing a simple forehand, to playing a topspin ground shot.
    - The initial motor programme is now just part of a more complicated motor programme with many more detailed subroutines.

Chapter 3 - MOTOR CONTROL OF SKILLS IN PHYSICAL EDUCATION

EXECUTIVE PROGRAMMES AND SUBROUTINES

To understand how motor programmes are formed one must examine hierarchies of control.

HIERARCHIES OF CONTROL

- A **hierarchy** is an order usually arranged in a pyramid shape.
  For example, the hierarchy of staff responsibilities in a school or company.
- A movement or sequence of movements can be arranged in a hierarchy.

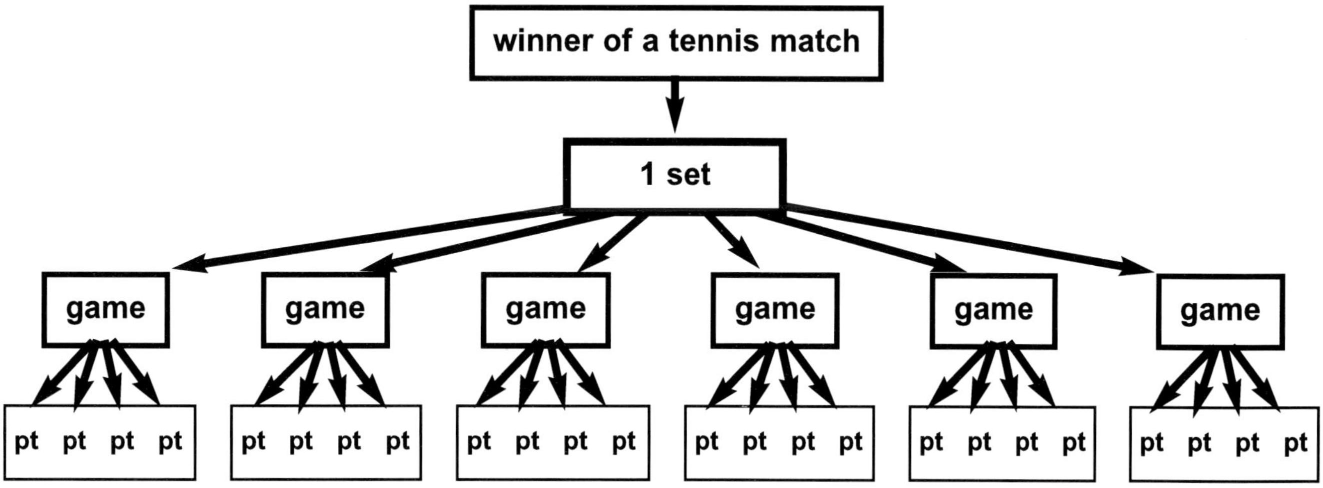

1. To be a winner the performer must win a set:
- To win a set, 6 games must be won.
- To win a game 4 points must be won.

2. To win a point the rally must be won:
- To win the rally number of shots must be played.

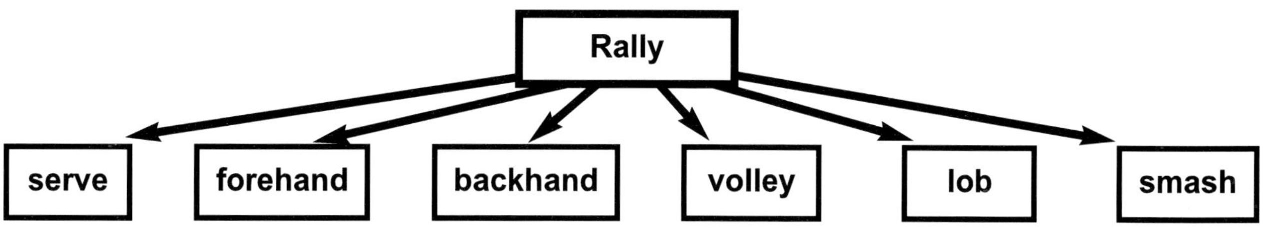

3. To play each stroke the performer must have mastered the points of correct stroke production.

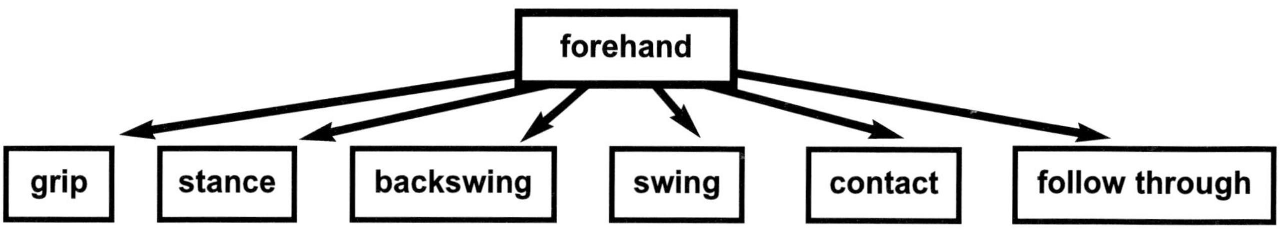

- **In order to be a winner the basics must have been fully learned, only then can the performer move onto the next step of the hierarchy.**

Chapter 3 - MOTOR CONTROL OF SKILLS IN PHYSICAL EDUCATION

LEARNING BY CONVERTING EXECUTIVE MOTOR PROGRAMMES INTO SUBROUTINES

- **First learning stage**:

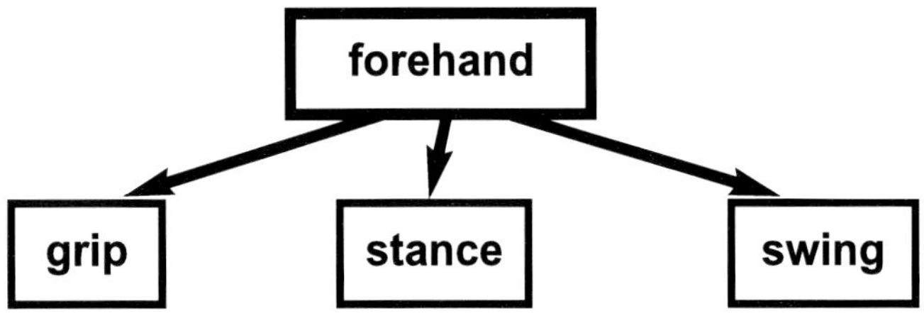

Executive Programme

subroutines

- **Second learning stage**:

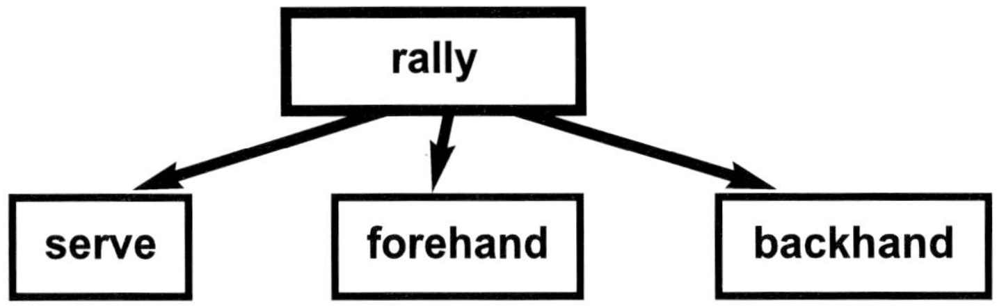

Executive Programme

subroutines

- Once the performer **learns** the forehand he / she will be able to put it into a rally. What once was an executive programme (**forehand**) now becomes a **subroutine** of a **more complex** executive programme.
- According to Robb **subroutines** are "**has-been**" **executive programmes**. A skill can be a **subroutine** for an **experienced** performer and an **executive programme** for the **learner**.
- It can be seen that we learn skills in **stages**. We must **fully learn** the **first stage** before moving on to a second stage.

IMPORTANCE TO THE TEACHER

- According to **Fitts and Posner**, adults learn new skills by **reorganising existing** subroutines. This implies that the performance of new skills is **dependent** on **previously learned subroutines**.
- The **early years** (between 8 and 12) have been seen as a very **important** time for **skill learning**. Subroutines learned during this time can have a **great effect** later on in life. It is therefore very important that **early skills** are **learned correctly**.
- To be able to move onto more complex skills the **young learner** must **first develop** a **number** of varied subroutines. This person cannot learn new and different skills if he / she does not have a similar subroutine to draw on.
- The teacher must ensure that the young learner develops a **wide variety** of **correctly** learned subroutines.
- The executive programme is concerned with the **correct timing** or **sequence** of the subroutines. Therefore, it is important that subroutines are learned in the **correct order**.
- The teacher must suggest the order in which the parts of a skill should be learned and **devise practices** which will enable the subroutines to **fit together** smoothly.

Chapter 3 - MOTOR CONTROL OF SKILLS IN PHYSICAL EDUCATION

MOTOR CONTROL

OPEN LOOP THEORY

Open loop theory is concerned with the sending of information.

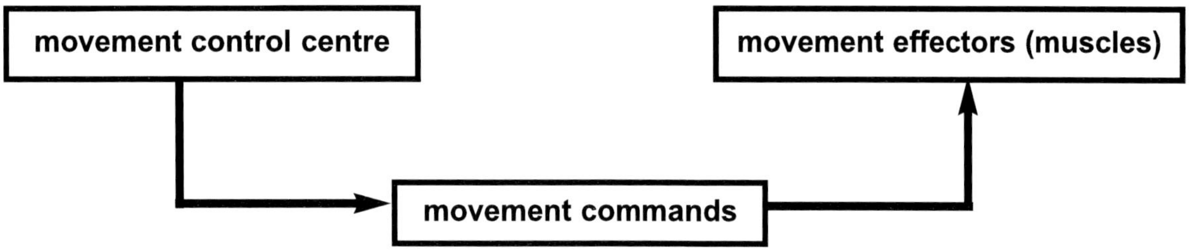

- **According to open loop theory** a **decision** to make a movement is made by the **movement control centre**. All the necessary **information** is sent in **one big chunk** (movement commands) to movement effectors (voluntary muscles).

- The information is received by the **effector organs** (voluntary muscles) which carry out the **movement**. **Feedback** is available but does **not** control movement. Because of this, movments are executed without any alterations due to sensory feedback.
  For example, a golf swing:
  - The brain assesses the situation.
  - The brain then sends commands to the voluntary muscles concerned with how to make the swing.
  - These voluntary muscles carry out the commands.

LIMITATIONS OF OPEN LOOP THEORY

- According to Schmidt, the brain **cannot store** millions upon millions of separate motor programmes. In addition the brain **cannot cope with new movements** for which it does **not have** a motor programme.

- Open loop theory explains how **fast movements** are acheived, but **cannot explain** how **slow positioning movements** are performed where it is apparent that the performer is able to change a movement half way through a motor programme.
  In this case, the movements probably involve the use of many mechanisms including open and closed loop systems (see next few pages).

Chapter 3 - MOTOR CONTROL OF SKILLS IN PHYSICAL EDUCATION

CLOSED LOOP THEORY

Closed loop theory is concerned with the importance of feedback.

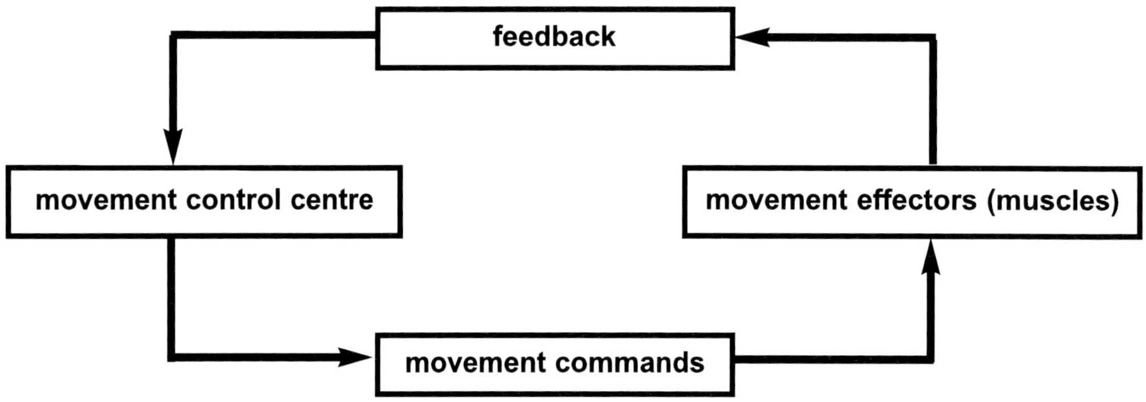

- **According to closed loop theory** a **decision** to make a movement is made by the movement control centre.

- But **not all of the information** necessary to make the movement is **sent** to the effector organs at once. The **rest** of the information is sent **during** the movement. The **amount and type** of information sent depends on the **feedback** received during the movement.

- Because of this **feedback**, changes can be made **during** the movement.

- **Closed loop theory** best explains how the brain deals with **slow positioning skills** or **balancing skills** like riding a bike.
  - When riding, the **brain** sends **messages** to the muscles concerning **how** to ride.
  - The **muscles** send **messages** back to the brain concerning the **performance**.
  - When the **brain detects any errors** in balance, it **sends further commands** to the muscles **to rectify** the imbalance.
  - Hence **feedback** seems to play an **important** part in such activities.

Chapter 3 - MOTOR CONTROL OF SKILLS IN PHYSICAL EDUCATION

DIFFERENCE BETWEEN OPEN AND CLOSED LOOP THEORY

- According to **closed loop theorists**, feedback can be used **during** movement. Movements can be **changed at any time**.

- According to **open loop theorists**, feedback **cannot be used during** movement, only afterwards. Once commands have been sent, the **movement cannot be changed** until the commands have been carried out.

- **Open loop theory** best explains the performing of fast movements where there is no time to react to feedback.
  For example, throwing, hitting and catching fast moving objects, jumping.

- **Closed loop theory** best explains the performing of slower movements where there is time to react to feedback.
  For example, positioning movements, hitting and catching slow moving objects.

TEACHING FOR CLOSED LOOP THEORY

- For **closed loop** movements the teacher will need to provide the learner with feedback which should include **knowledge of performance** and **knowledge of results**. The learner's own **kinaesthetic feedback** can be **enhanced** by the teacher asking how the movement **felt**.

TEACHING FOR OPEN LOOP THEORY

- Teaching for **open loop theory** is concerned with providing the learner with enough information and helping the learner to send the information in the **correct order** (the timing of the movement). This can be achieved by providing **large amounts of varied practice**. This **increases movement memory** and so increases the chance of the correct motor commands being sent when performing a new skill.

- **Learning skills in parts** to give the learner an idea of which order to run the parts (subroutines) of the skill. This will help to improve timing and coordination.

- In the **early stages of learning** there is **no spare attentional capacity**. Consequently, it is **difficult** for the learner to use **ongoing feedback** during the movement.
  It can be assumed at this stage, **learning** could be best explained using **open loop theory**.

- In the **later stages of learning**, when **spare attentional capacity** is available, the learner could use concurrent feedback.
  At this stage **learning** could be explained using **both theories**.

Chapter 3 - MOTOR CONTROL OF SKILLS IN PHYSICAL EDUCATION

SCHEMA THEORY (Schmidt) (1975)

- A **Schema** is the **stored information** needed to make a **decision** or **movement**. Movements are the result of **motor programmes**. A **motor programme** contains **all the information** needed to make a **movement**.
  For example:
  - Which muscles to use.
  - The order of the muscles to be used.
  - The phasing of contractions of the muscles.
  - Or how long in-between each contraction.

- According to Schmidt, the brain **cannot store millions upon millions** of separate motor programmes. In addition, the brain **cannot cope with new movements** for which it does not have a motor programme. Instead of separate motor programmes for every movement, Schmidt asserts that **motor programmes are grouped together** to form **generalised motor programmes**, each of which would provide a **schema**.
  For example, a generalised motor programme for:
  - Jumping.
  - Throwing.
  - Kicking.
  - Lifting.

- According to schema theory, the brain does **not have to store so many programmes** and any new movement can probably be executed by running a **generalised motor programme** which closely matches the requirements of the new movement.

- The bigger the **generalised motor programme** (**GMP**) the more efficient the movement is likely to be. The **size** of the **GMP** can be increased by gaining **new experiences**. When performing a **new skill** the performer draws on **previous experience**.
  A **large GMP** is likely to contain information related to a **very similar task** so the performer is more likely to perform the new task successfully.

- According to Schema Theory, **successful completion of a task** depends on the **size** of the **GMP**. The **GMP** can be **increased** or **strengthened** in a number of ways.

Chapter 3 - MOTOR CONTROL OF SKILLS IN PHYSICAL EDUCATION

SCHEMA THEORY (continued)

- Large amounts of **varied practice** are needed to improve or **strengthen the schema** for a skill. The performer should attempt to **practice** the skill in a number of **different ways.**
  For example:
  - A basketball player should practice jump shots and set shots from all parts of the key.
  - The performer is more likely to successfully make a shot in the game because he / she has practised the same shot in training.

- The sports performer should also **learn** a number of **different skills** from different activities. This will **increase the likelihood** of the performer being able to **perform a new skill**, as he / she will be able to transfer knowledge gained from practising a wide range of different skills. It is important that any new skill is learned **correctly**.
  The performer will want to have correct information (and as little incorrect information as possible) in the schema, as it will affect the performance of other skills.

- **Extrinsic feedback** is important as it is used to **correct and update** the schema. The coach should provide the performer with infomation about the performance in order for him / her to update the schema. The coach should also help the performer **selectively attend** to the most appropriate feedback.

- When performing a **new task**, the performer needs to use information from **previous similar tasks**. **Errors** are helpful because the bigger the bank of old information, the bigger the chance of selecting the correct response for the new task. **Errors are helpful** because they help to **strengthen** the schema.
  For example, canoeing:
  - How does the canoeist know how far he / she can lean before the canoe capsizes?
  - The canoeist knows because he / she has capsized accidentally before.

Chapter 3 - MOTOR CONTROL OF SKILLS IN PHYSICAL EDUCATION

THE FORMATION OF SCHEMA

Information used to form schema includes:

Initial Conditions	Information concerning the **environment**. For example: Where are team-mates, opposition, the goal? What are the playing conditions and weather? What is the condition of the car, horse or boat?
Response Specifications	Information concerning **how to perform** a movement. For example: How much speed is needed? How much force is needed? How big should the movement size be? Which technique should be used?
Movement Outcomes	Information concerning the **success or failure** of the movement. For example: What was the result of the performance? How far, how fast, how well, how many?
Sensory Consequences	Information concerning **how the movement felt**.

There are two types of schema: **recall schema** and **recognition schema**.

RECALL SCHEMA (initial conditions and response specifications)

- A **recall schema** contains all the information required **before** a motor programme is selected and run.
- A **recall schema** is formed when the **initial conditions** are combined with the **response specifications** to initiate a motor programme.

RECOGNITION SCHEMA (movement outcomes and sensory consequences)

- A **recognition schema** contains all the information needed to **make corrections to faulty performance** and **remember correct performance**.
- During and after any performance the schema is strengthened by **2 types of information**.
- **Information** from **movement outcomes** and **sensory consequences** (the feelings and information from the senses about a performance) is **combined** to form **Recognition Schema**. If the performance was correct it needs to be remembered - if it was incorrect, adjustments will be made to movement parameters.

CONCLUSIONS

- According to Schmidt, a **recall schema** is used for **quick ballistic movements** when there is not enough time to process feedback.
- A **recognition schema** is used for **evaluating performance** or for **producing slow movements** when there is enough time to process feedback.
- Schema theory can be used to explain all movement.
- **Slow movements** can be explained using **closed loop theory**, whilst **fast movements** can only be explained using **open loop theory**.

Chapter 4 - LEARNING SKILLS IN PHYSICAL EDUCATION

Chapter 4 - LEARNING SKILLS IN PHYSICAL EDUCATION

MOTIVATION AND AROUSAL

MOTIVATION

According to Stallings (1966), motivation is an **internal factor** that **arouses** and **directs** behaviour.

- **Motivation** is the **power** or **drive** behind why we do something.
- **Motivation** is responsible for:
  - The **selection** and **preference** for an activity.
  - The **persistence** at the activity.
  - The **intensity** and **effort** put into performance.

TYPES OF MOTIVATION

❒ **Intrinsic motivation**	Feelings from **inside** ourselves. For example: Fun. Enjoyment. Joy. Satisfaction.
❒ **Extrinsic motivation**	Feelings coming from gaining **external rewards**. **Physical** (money, trophies). **Emotional** (praise).
❒ **Primary motivation**	Derived from the activity **itself**.
❒ **Secondary motivation**	Comes from **anything other than taking part**. For example: For coach. Friends. Medals.

- Any aspect of competing can have a **positive** or **negative** effect on motivation.
- **Winning** is **positively** motivating, **losing** can be **negatively** motivating.
- An **audience** can have both a **positive** and **negative** effect on performance.

Chapter 4 - LEARNING SKILLS IN PHYSICAL EDUCATION

INTRINSIC OR EXTRINSIC MOTIVATION - WHICH IS MOST EFFECTIVE?

Intrinsic motivation can outlast extrinsic motivation.

- Athletes who are too old or unfit to win trophies, fame or money, may still be able to **enjoy** sport.
- Once an athlete has won a gold medal what else is there?
  Enjoyment is the best reason for taking part in sport.

The type of motivation required depends on the task.

- Margaret Clifford (1972), "As **task complexity** increases **intrinsic motivation** increases." The learning of complex tasks is heavily dependent upon intrinsic motivation. Consequently, **simple tasks** may be performed more often to a higher standard if **external rewards** are present.
- Tasks which athletes **do not wish** to complete (scary, fear, risk of injury) may be completed with the use of **extrinsic** rewards.

The regular use of extrinsic rewards may undermine intrinsic motivation.

- Sport that is viewed as **play** may be transformed **into work** (with all the **negative feelings** of burden) if rewards are given for performance.
  When the **rewards are taken away** there may **no** longer be any **reason** to **take part**.

Motivation is greatest when the athlete is in control of the situation.

- Situations can be internally or externally controlled.
  If you do something because you **want to** (**internal control**) your level of motivation will be **higher** than if you are **told to do something** (**external control**). Extrinsic motivation can increase external control whilst intrinsic motivation can increase internal control.
- **Extrinsic** motivation can **turn play into work**. The use of extrinsic rewards may increase external control.
  For example, the athlete who used to train for intrinsic reasons but is then given extrinsic rewards. He / she may not train at all when the rewards are taken away, feeling that the only motivation for training previously had been the receipt of extrinsic rewards.
- **Rewards** should be used **very carefully**.
  Rewards should be used as a means of informing the athlete about how well he / she is doing rather than being used as the motivation for competing. They should be used to **complement** and **heighten intrinsic motivation** rather than as a controlling factor determining whether or not to do something.

Chapter 4 - LEARNING SKILLS IN PHYSICAL EDUCATION

DRIVE REDUCTION THEORY

- **Drive reduction theory** can be used to explain **how learning takes place**. **Learning** can be the outcome of a need to **satisfy** a **desire** or **drive**. In the sporting context a desire or **drive** may result from a **need to succeed**, **improve**, to **gain pleasure** or **power**.

- If a person has these desires or drives, he / she will try to find ways to **satisfy** them. The performer will **try different ways** to satisfy or **reduce** the drive. In this way the performer will eventually become **more skilful** as a result of trying to satisfy the drives. But at the same time is **not satisfied by repeating the same** skill or **performance**, only by achieving a newer **more desirable** / complex / advanced skill or **performance**.
  Hence **drive is reduced** (motivation is less) to **repeat the original skill**.

  For example:
  - A rock climber who is driven to climb a certain route.
  - He / she will persevere and learn new ways to overcome the problems of the climb, just because of the expected pleasure of reaching the top.
  - But will then not be as satisfied by attempting the same route next time.

Key areas of the theory:

- Drives are arranged in a **hierarchy** from strongest to weakest.
- Subjects will try hardest to satisfy the **strongest** drives.
- Learning takes place by **connecting** a **stimulus** (drive) with a **particular response**, forming an **S-R bond**.
- With continued **practice** the **S-R bond** is **strengthened** and a **habit** is **established**.
- As the subject becomes technically more proficient the drive becomes increasingly **more satisfied**. This **reduces the likelihood** of further attempts to improve since the satisfaction of drive causes a **reduction in drive** in the future.
  What is the point in playing an opponent who has already been beaten a number of times before?
  This phenomenon is known as **inhibition** (the reduction in drive or motivation as a result of successful performance).
- A **coach** should reduce the likelihood of inhibition by **maintaining drive**. If a person is motivated by **winning** in **difficult** situations and is faced with an opponent he / she has beaten several times before, the coach should try to make the situation more challenging by handicapping the strong player or by giving the weaker player an advantage.

Teachers can apply drive theory in a number of ways:

- Make a task become **more important** in the learner's eyes. Or make the task **match** the learner's **own desires** or drive. Make it competitive, difficult or fun.
- Keep the learner **focused** on the task and ensure he / she realises how the task can be used to satisfy his / her own desires. Students need to know "what's in it for them."
- Reduce the chances of inhibition by maintaining **high levels of challenge**.

Chapter 4 - LEARNING SKILLS IN PHYSICAL EDUCATION

THE RELATIONSHIP BETWEEN AROUSAL AND PERFORMANCE

AROUSAL

Arousal can be defined as the **state of activation** or **excitement** a person has in any situation.

- In general, **too much** or **too little** arousal can **adversely** affect performance. The coach will need to manipulate the athlete's level of arousal in order to **maximise** performance. The coach must **manipulate** arousal levels in order to find the **optimum** level of arousal for any personality type performing any activity.

- Two main theories best explain the relationship between arousal and performance:
  - **Inverted "U"** Theory.
  - **Hull's Drive** Theory.

THE INVERTED 'U' THEORY

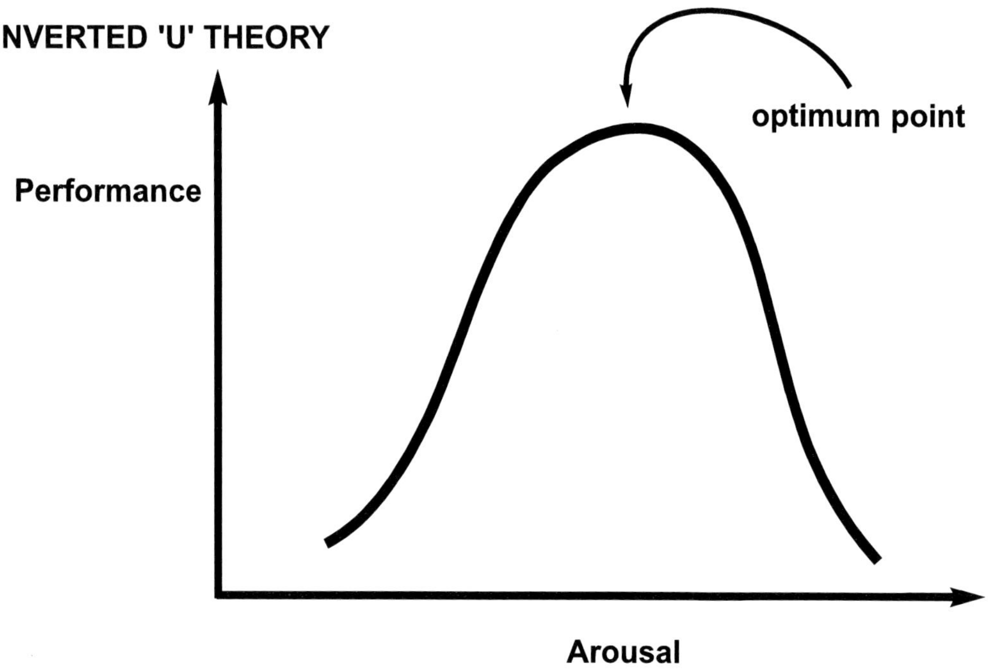

In this theory:

- **Performance increases** with increasing levels of **arousal** up to a point (the **optimum** point).
  After this point, **increasing** levels of **arousal** brings about **decreasing** levels of performance.

- The **optimum point** marks out the most beneficial level of arousal for any task. It can change depending on the **task**, level of **learning** and **personality** of the performer.

- The coach will try to get the athlete to the optimum point, and arouse but **not over-arouse** the athlete .

Chapter 4 - LEARNING SKILLS IN PHYSICAL EDUCATION

HULL'S DRIVE THEORY

This is an alternative to the Inverted 'U' theory.

❒ The term "**drive**" is linked directly to the performer's **level of arousal**. **Drive Theory** states that **performance increases** with **increasing** levels of **arousal** so the more arousal the better the performance.

❒ However, Hull added that this would only be the case if the **skill** had previously been **well-learned**. Performance levels for a **beginner** would **reduce** with increasing levels of arousal. This theory explains why, for many beginners, it is easy to perform a skill when there is no pressure, but when pressure is introduced, mistakes start to be made. Alternatively an increase in pressure can actually help the **skilled athlete** perform to the **best** of his / her ability.

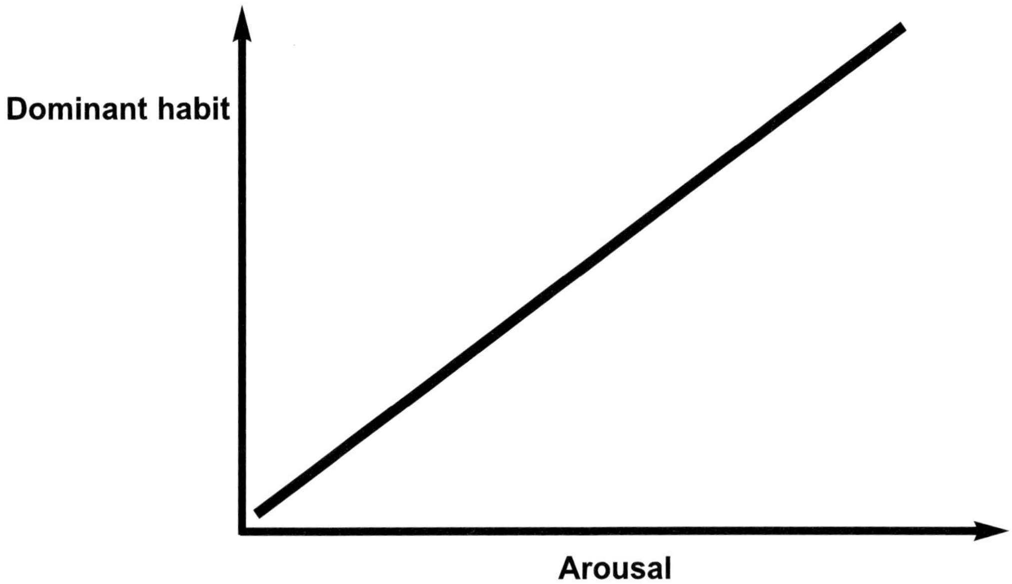

According to **Hull's** Drive theory: **Performance = Habit x Drive**

❒ **Habit** refers to the **strength of the learned response** or skill, and whether the **correct response** has been practised until it has become **habitualised**. Any response can have a strong or weak habit depending on the **level of practice** at that skill.
Drive refers to the performer's **level of arousal**.

❒ **Increased levels** of arousal are said to bring about the **dominant response** (strongest from a number of possibilities).

❒ For the **novice**, the dominant response is usually **incorrect**, due to him / her performing habitual movements which are inaccurate (insufficient learning of the correct movements). For the **experienced performer** the dominant response is usually **correct** due to the skill being well-practised and more habitualised.

❒ Until a **skill** has been **well-learned** any increase in arousal will probably result in a decrease in performance. Once a skill is **fully learned**, increased arousal is more likely to cause increased performance.

Chapter 4 - LEARNING SKILLS IN PHYSICAL EDUCATION

OPTIMUM LEVELS OF AROUSAL

The optimum level of arousal is dependent on a number of factors including **task difficulty, type of task, level of learning** and **personality**.

- For **simple** skills, the learner will need to be **more aroused** than for **complex** skills. If the task is **simple**, it is easy for the performer to become disinterested. Higher levels of arousal will ensure greater concentration.

- **Complex** skills require large amounts of **attentional capacity** and so require lower levels of arousal. **Excessive arousal** can cause frustration and narrowing of attentional focus (tunnel vision). This can be detrimental to performance.

- **High** levels of **arousal** for **fine motor skills** such as those found in snooker, can be **detrimental** to performance due to unwanted increases in muscle tension. **Gross motor skills** such as those found in weight lifting require relatively higher levels of arousal than for fine motor skills.

- **Hazardous** activities will require high levels of arousal.

- During the **early stages of learning**, arousal levels need to be relatively low. **Too much arousal** can affect the learner's ability to attend to information. At **later stages of learning**, when the learner has spare attentional capacity, greater levels of arousal can help motivate the performer.

- **Personality** can affect optimum arousal levels. The **introvert** may find it easy to become **over-aroused** whilst the **extrovert** will **need increased** levels of **arousal** to reach the optimum point. If the performer requires greater levels of arousal to reach the optimum point, then the inverted 'U' curve is shifted to the right as shown below.

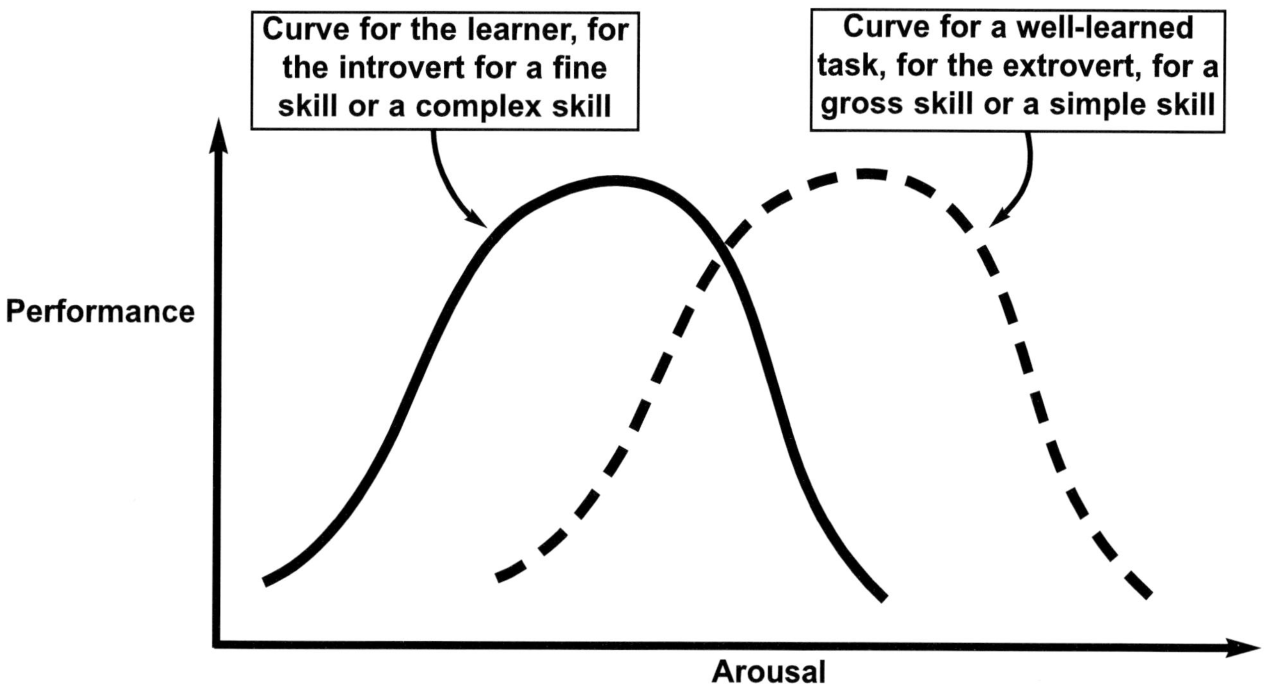

Chapter 4 - LEARNING SKILLS IN PHYSICAL EDUCATION

TEACHING FOR MOTIVATION

- Find out the performer's **reason to participate** and adapt teaching methods to accommodate for it.
  For example, if the performer is motivated by competition, make training more competitive.
- **Success** is motivating. Ensure everyone gets his or her fair share of success.
- **Praise** is motivating. Make certain that correct behaviour is rewarded.
- **Play** itself is motivating. Training sessions should include the opportunity to play.
- Similar training sessions can be boring. Ensure training is **varied** and **different**.
- Each activity has an **optimum** level of motivation.
  For example, to compete in dangerous sports the performer must be highly motivated. The teacher must be aware of the optimum level of motivation needed for any activity and try to help the performer achieve it.
- The **overuse of extrinsic rewards** can turn play into work when the performer starts to perceive the reward as being the only reason to play.
- Make the performer seek high levels of achievement by increasing his / her **need to succeed**. The high achiever sets **high yet achievable goals**, is confident and positive and attributes success to his / her own skill.

MEASURING MOTIVATION

1. Tutko and Richards (1972) Motivational Rating Scale

This inventory attempted to measure 11 traits which contribute to the motivation of highly successful athletes:

Aggression	**Mental Toughness**	**Responsibility**
Coachability	**Drive**	**Trust**
Emotional Control	**Self confidence**	**Conscientiousness**
Determination	**Leadership**	

2. Kenyon (1968) Attitude Towards Physical Activity Inventory

This test identified and measured 6 reasons why people take part in physical activity:

Social	**Vertigo (excitement)**	**Ascetic (physical challenge)**
Heath and Fitness	**Aesthetic**	**Catharsis (relaxation)**

3. Alderman and Wood (1976) Incentive Motivation Inventory

This inventory attempted to measure 7 reasons why people take part in physical activity:

Affiliation	**Independence**	**Stress**
Aggression	**Power**	**Success**
Excellence		

Chapter 5 - THEORIES RELATING TO THE LEARNING OF MOVEMENT SKILLS

Chapter 5 - THEORIES RELATING TO THE LEARNING OF MOVEMENT SKILLS

The following theories offer three contrasting views on how motor skills are learned.

ASSOCIATIONALIST / CONNECTIONIST THEORY OF LEARNING

- **Associationalist** theory is sometimes called
    - **Connectionist** theory or.
    - **Behaviourist** theory.

  This theory asserts that learning takes place as a consequence of the **connection** between a **stimulus** and a **response**.

- A **stimulus** is an **incentive** or **spur**, an action or event that **provokes** an **action in response** to the stimulus.

- The **connection** between a stimulus and a response is an outcome of conditioning. **Conditioning** is a form of training whose purpose is to make behaviour habitualised (unvarying - and a learnt habit).

- **Learning** involves a **change in behaviour**. Learning takes place when a **connection** between a **stimulus** and **response** is made, the **S-R bond**.
  For example, when playing cricket:
    - If a player is hurt when trying to make a catch or play a shot.
    - Then he / she will avoid trying to make a catch or play a shot in future.
    - The coach will try to **change behaviour** by **persuading** the learner to connect:
        - The stimulus of a cricket ball in close proximity.
        - To the new response of catching (fielder) or playing a shot (batter).
    - The coach will **train** or condition the **learner** until the **preferred response is habitual**.

  The method by which this is accomplished is that explained using the theories of **classical** and **operant** conditioning.

Chapter 5 - THEORIES RELATING TO THE LEARNING OF MOVEMENT SKILLS

CLASSICAL CONDITIONING

- **Classical conditioning** is concerned with the **stimulus-response** bond.

- The performer does **not make a decision** towards the stimulus, since all responses are **automatic**.

- In most textbooks, **Pavlov's dogs** experiment is used to explain classical conditioning:
    - Pavlov found that when dogs were given food (**stimulus**), they unsurprisingly salivated (**response**).
    - Pavlov was able to demonstrate that learning had taken place by **conditioning** the dogs to salivate when faced with a **alternative stimulus**, a bell.
    - The bell was rung every time the dogs were fed.
    - Eventually the dogs salivated (**response**) when the bell was rung without the presence of food (**stimulus**).

- It is very difficult to teach using the classical conditioning approach, since most sporting situations require some element of choice. Classical conditioning perhaps could be used to teach **set drills and practices** (without any variation - fixed in feel and content) which **connect** particular **stimuli** to particular **responses** without thought.

- Strictly speaking, classical conditioning only applies where the **response is reflexive** and **without** any **conscious thought**. Examples of such reflexes would be:
    - Blinking when a sudden movement threatens the face.
    - Turning away or jumping when a ball is shot directly at the head.
    - Withdrawing a hand which is stamped on.

- **Reinforcement** is necessary to **strengthen** the S-R bond.

- **Learning** through **set drills** may be quick but does **not ensure** that students **understand** the purpose of movements, or the possible integration with other similar skills.

Chapter 5 - THEORIES RELATING TO THE LEARNING OF MOVEMENT SKILLS

OPERANT CONDITIONING

- **Operant conditioning** is concerned with the **stimulus-response** bond.
- Operant means a **behaviour**, so **operant conditioning** is the **training of a behaviour**.
- **Skinner's box** experiment demonstrated how behaviour could be **modified** by conditioning:
    - A rat was placed in a special box.
    - The rat learned to connect or associate the sound of food coming down a shute to the delivery of food to a food tray.
    - The rat responded by moving to the food tray.
    - The new behaviour to be learned was the connection of gaining food not by listening for a sound but by pressing a lever.
    - The rat was rewarded when behaviour came **close** to the **desired response** (rat moved towards lever or lifted a paw).
    - Through **trial and error** the rat eventually pushed the lever and was rewarded by food.
    - Through practice the rat learned to connect the **stimulus of feeling hungry** to the **response of pushing a lever**.
    - The rat performed the action because it thought it would be **rewarded** with food.
- The **learner**, when faced with a **stimulus**, will have to **choose** from a number of **different responses.**
- The learner **makes a decision** based on the idea that a **particular response** will be **rewarded**.
  For example, a team games player in possession of the ball must decide whether to shoot, pass or dribble.
  The eventual response is dependent on the expectation on the performer's part of the response being **rewarded**.
- The **teacher** wants the performer to pick the correct response to a stimulus and ensures that this happens by rewarding the performer for **connecting** the **correct response** to the **stimulus** and **punishing** the performer when the **wrong connection** is made.
  For example, the games player who always dribbles rather than passes:
    - Will need to be **rewarded** for passing.
    - Be **deterred** from dribbling.
    - In order to **weaken** an existing, **incorrect S-R bond**.
    - And **establish** a **new S-R bond**.
- The learner may not know why the response is correct only that it will be **rewarded**.
- For the **reward** to be effective it must **closely follow the response**.
- Teaching through operant conditioning must include **positive reinforcement** and **reward**. This is the main way the S-R bond is **strengthened**. Learning may take place through **trial and error**, which involves trying to **link** a correct response to a stimulus using random acts.
  For example, in badminton:
    - An opponent plays an overhead clear to your midcourt stroke (stimulus).
    - After experimentation you find that the best reply would be to smash (response).
- When teaching through **operant conditioning** the teacher must try to **strengthen the desired S-R bond** and **weaken** an **inappropriate S-R bond**. The teacher should use **positive reinforcement** (reward) to **strengthen correct response**, and use negative reinforcement or punishment on the learner who has connected an inappropriate response to a stimulus.

Chapter 5 - THEORIES RELATING TO THE LEARNING OF MOVEMENT SKILLS

COGNITIVE THEORY OF LEARNING

- **Cognitive** theorists argue that the **learner has a part to play** in his / her own learning. The **learner** does **not thoughtlessly respond** to a stimulus as asserted by Classical Conditioning Theory. The **cognitive theory** of learning asserts that learning results from drawing on information from relevant variables in order to gain an **understanding** of the "whole picture".

- **Gestalt** is a word associated with cognitive theory.
  - **Gestalt** is the German for "**form**" or "**shape**".
  - To ensure **optimum learning** the learner must have access to "the big picture".
  - It is not good enough to be taught how to complete a particular skill if the learner does not know when, where and why he / she is using the skill.
  - **Gestaltists** believe that learning takes place when the learner **understands** the problem faced (such as details of how the learning of a new skill is to be undertaken).

- In order to **understand** the problem (of learning a skill), the learner must have information about the whole situation and must be able to draw on **previous experience** and **knowledge**.

- Theorists use the term **intervening variables** to describe the **influencing factors** (variables) which come between (intervene) a stimulus occurring and a response being selected.

- In order to make a response the learner will need to **assess the variables** and decide upon a course of action.
  For example, a basketball player receiving a pass:
  - Will decide whether to shoot, pass or dribble.
  - Only after assessing the intervening variables such as:
    - His / her position on court.
    - The position of team mates.
    - The positions of opposition players.

Chapter 5 - THEORIES RELATING TO THE LEARNING OF MOVEMENT SKILLS

COGNITIVE THEORY OF LEARNING (continued)

Understanding "The Big Picture"

- The performer can only assess the intervening variables if he / she **understands** the present task and can relate it to **past experience**. It is important that the learner gains an idea of the **whole problem** rather than the task's constituent parts.
  For example, volleyball tactics:
  - The problem is how to play an attacking shot after receiving a serve.
  - The answer is to play the ball to the front of the court.
  - Then play the ball high to a net player who can hit it downwards over the net.
  - By presenting the problem as a whole, players will understand the purpose of the "dig", "volley" and "spike."
  - Teaching the spike by itself has little purpose if the learner never gets chance to use it because the ball never gets played to the front of the court.

- If a skill is taught in isolation the learner understands what the skill consists of, and how to do it, but not why or when to use it.

Using Past Experience

- The process by which learners use **past experience** to help them solve problems is known as **insight learning**.
  For example:
  - A badminton player uses badminton experience when playing other racquet sports.
  - A footballer can easily learn hockey because the principles of play for each sport are very similar.
  - An A level student can use knowledge from the course to understand:
    - Why he / she cannot play sport at maximum intensity for long periods.
    - Why the performance of a learner decreases with an audience present,.
    - Why boys or girls may be unwilling to participate in certain activities.

- **Cognitive theorists** or Gestaltists believe in the **learner appreciating** and understanding the **whole problem**. It is important for the learner to draw from as **many learning experiences** as possible, in order to enable him / her to analyse the intervening variables and gain **insight** into the final solution.

Chapter 5 - THEORIES RELATING TO THE LEARNING OF MOVEMENT SKILLS

SOCIAL LEARNING THEORY

- This section looks at the effects that **people** can have on **behaviour** and **performance**.

- According to **Social Learning Theory** (**SLT**) all behaviour is **learned**. The greatest amount of learning takes place at an early age through **socialisation**.
  Socialisation is the process by which society **trains** its children to behave like adults.

- Through **socialisation** we **learn**:
  - The **correct patterns of behaviour** (norms).
  - What is **right** and **wrong** (values).
  - Our **status** and **role** in society.

- Physical Education and Sport can act as **part of** the **socialisation** process. It helps to transmit the norms and values of society.
  Sport is seen as developing values such as:
  - Fair play.
  - Tolerance.
  - Co-operation.
  - Teamwork.
  - Determination.

- According to **SLT** we learn what our behaviour should be through the processes of **observational learning** and **modelling**.

- **Observational Learning**:
  - People can learn merely by **observing** the **behaviour** of **others**.

- **Modelling**:
  - A person can learn behaviours by **observing a model perform**.
  - For modelling to work the model's performance must be **correct**.
  - The **model** must have **high status** or competency in order for observers to want to copy the model's behaviour.
  - The **task** must be seen as **relevant** to the performer.
  - Modelling behaviour is more likely if the model is the **same age or gender** as the observer.

Chapter 5 - THEORIES RELATING TO THE LEARNING OF MOVEMENT SKILLS

BANDURA'S MODEL OF OBSERVATIONAL LEARNING

According to **Bandura** (1977), learning takes place because the observer is able to **correct sensory images** and arrange them in time order (temporally) so that they make sense.

The model has 4 stages:

Attention Processes

- This stage is concerned with the aspects of the model's performance upon which the learner needs to **concentrate** or attend.
- Because the learner has **limited attentional capacity**, he / she will need to use **selective attention** to pick out the **relevant cues**.
- A teacher will need to highlight the **relevant** cues.

Retention Processes

- This stage involves the performer attempting to **remember important parts** of the model's performance.
- **Repeated demonstrations** help retention, as does **mental rehearsal**.

Motor Reproduction

- This involves the performer attempting to **copy** the model's performance.
- The learner's performance can be improved with **practice** and through the use of both **intrinsic** and **extrinsic feedback**.

Motivational Processes

- This stage is concerned with the **reasons why** the learner **wants to copy** the model's performance.
- For the learner to **want to copy** the model's performance, he / she must have a reason.
- The **status of the model** can affect motivation.
- The **importance of the task** will also affect motivation.

Chapter 6 - REINFORCEMENT

Chapter 6 - REINFORCEMENT

REINFORCEMENT AND PUNISHMENT

This section is concerned with how a coach can induce a performer to **repeat a correct performance**.

- According to theories related to the S-R bond, **reinforcement** is necessary to **strengthen the bond** and improve learning.

- **Magill** (1989): "**Reinforcement** is any action or event that **increases the probability** of a **response** occurring again".

POSITIVE AND NEGATIVE REINFORCEMENT

- Examples of **positive reinforcement** are **praise** and **rewards**. If a performer receives praise or rewards he / she is more likely to repeat the act in expectation of future rewards.

- **Negative reinforcement** is the **removal of praise** when performance is **incorrect**. A performer **wants** to be rewarded, if he / she is not rewarded then he / she will change his / her performance in order to increase the chances of being rewarded.

- **Negative reinforcement** can also involve the coach **punishing incorrect performance** and **saying nothing** when performance is **correct**. The performer will want to avoid being scolded and will try to achieve correct performance.

PUNISHMENT

- **Magill** (1989): "**Punishment** is any action or event that **decreases the probability** of a **response** occurring again".

- **Punishment** is **different** from **reinforcement**. **Reinforcement** tells the performer **what to do**. **Punishment** tells the performer **what not to do**. Consequently reinforcement is more useful than punishment.
  Punishment is doing something **unpleasant** to the performer when he / she **performs incorrectly** or indulges in **inappropriate behaviour**.

- Praise is also better than punishment because **punishment** can lead to **negative feelings** such as anxiety and resistant behaviour.

WHEN AND HOW TO USE REINFORCEMENT AND PUNISHMENT

- Reinforcement and punishment only work if they have an **important effect** on the performer or if the performer **perceives** the effect to be **important**. If the **coach** is **not respected** the reinforcement will be of no value.

- Reinforcement or punishment must **follow behaviour as soon as possible** if it is to be effective.

- If reinforcement is **overused** it loses its value.

- Reinforcement should only be used when observing **correct behaviour**.

Chapter 6 - REINFORCEMENT

THORNDIKE'S LAWS (1932)

Thorndike's laws can be used to used to explain **how and why** reinforcement and punishment works. These laws also can be used as methods to strengthen the S-R bond.

THORNDIKE'S LAW OF EFFECT

- **"Any action that is positively reinforced will tend to be repeated."**
- The learner **gains satisfaction** from being rewarded and will probably **want to repeat the action** in order to receive another reward. The same principle applies to punishment. An action that is **punished** could result in **annoyance**. The performer will **avoid repetition** of an **incorrect** action in order to **avoid** the **annoyance** associated with punishment.
- Rushall (1967) used punishment to annoy swimmers into producing correct performance.
    - The coach shone a torch into the face of a swimmer every time the swimmer committed a technical error.
    - The swimmer concentrated on performing correctly in order to avoid the annoyance of the torchlight.
- The **S-R bond is strengthened** by **rewarding the connection of a stimulus** to a **preferred response.**

THORNDIKE'S LAW OF READINESS

- A learner is **ready to perform** a motor skill only when he / she has the **capability** to perform the motor skill. This would be either through **physical maturity** (strength, speed, agility, stamina) or by **developing fundamental skills** and adapting them to perform a new skill.
  For example, to perform a triple jump a learner first needs to have mastered running, hopping, stepping and jumping.
- Thorndike states that when the learner has prepared him / herself to perform a skill, **completion of the skill** will bring **satisfaction**. Conversely, if the learner has not prepared him / herself, the **resultant failure** will result in **annoyance**.
- **Skills** need to be learned in **stages**. The teacher must ensure the most **basic of skills are fully learned** before covering more advanced skills. Learning can take place by **chaining (linking) simple skills** together to form more complex skills. The concept seems very similar to the way executive motor programmes are relegated to become subroutines of more complex executive programmes.

THORNDIKE'S LAW OF EXERCISE

- In simple terms **practice makes permanent. Repetition** strengthens the S-R bond thereby **increasing the habit** and increasing the likelihood of the performer **remembering** the **correct response** to a stimulus.
- Remember that **practice makes permanent**, not practice makes perfect. Practising the **incorrect response** to a stimulus will only help the performer learn **bad habits**.

Chapter 6 - REINFORCEMENT

Chapter 7 - PHASES OF MOVEMENT SKILL LEARNING

Chapter 7 - PHASES OF MOVEMENT SKILL LEARNING

PHASES OF MOVEMENT SKILL LEARNING

In order to learn any new skill the learner will pass through **three distinct phases** before achieving mastery of the skill.

COGNITIVE STAGE (absolute beginner)

- The learner needs to know **what to do**. He / she needs to get a **mental picture** of the movement. The teacher should make good use of **demonstrations**. **Visual information** best helps the learner gain the mental picture.

- The teacher uses **verbal cues** to highlight the correct sequencing of the movement. For example, the teacher says "now" to initiate the correct timing of a particular movement.

- The learner has a **limited attentional capacity** to cope with information. **Instructions** should be **brief** and to the point. **Too much information** will only **confuse** the learner.

- Since the learner has little idea of what is a correct performance, the teacher may have to use **physical guidance** and actually physically manipulate the learner's limbs into the correct position.

ASSOCIATIVE STAGE (fault correction)

- The learner now has an **overall picture** of what is required but **still makes mistakes**.

- The learner needs to know **how to complete each stage** of movement. The teacher may **break the skill into parts** and practice each part separately.

- The teacher will use **demonstration** to highlight **correct** technique and timing and use **verbal feedback** to correct faults. The learner will also need **encouragement** from the teacher in order to maintain motivation.

AUTONOMOUS STAGE (automatic)

- The learner knows how to complete the skill and can do so with a **great degree of competence**. The learner does not have to concentrate on performance and seems to **perform automatically**.

- The learner has **spare attentional capacity** and can now concentrate on other things. For example, in a team game a player can now concentrate on tactics.

- The learner has the **ability to teach him / herself**. The teacher can use quite **complicated verbal feedback** since the learner is capable of understanding it.

- The learner can make greater use of **kinaesthetic information**. The teacher should ask the learner to try and remember the **feeling** of a **correct movement**.

Chapter 7 - PHASES OF MOVEMENT SKILL LEARNING

ASSESSING LEARNING USING LEARNING CURVES

- **Learning** is a **change in performance** which is exhibited through increased levels of **consistency**.

- Learning can be **measured** through **performance tests**. The procedure is:
  - Test performance.
  - Practice.
  - Test again.
  - Practice.
  - Test again.

  If **learning** has taken place, **performance** should have **improved**.

DIFFERENT TYPES OF LEARNING CURVES

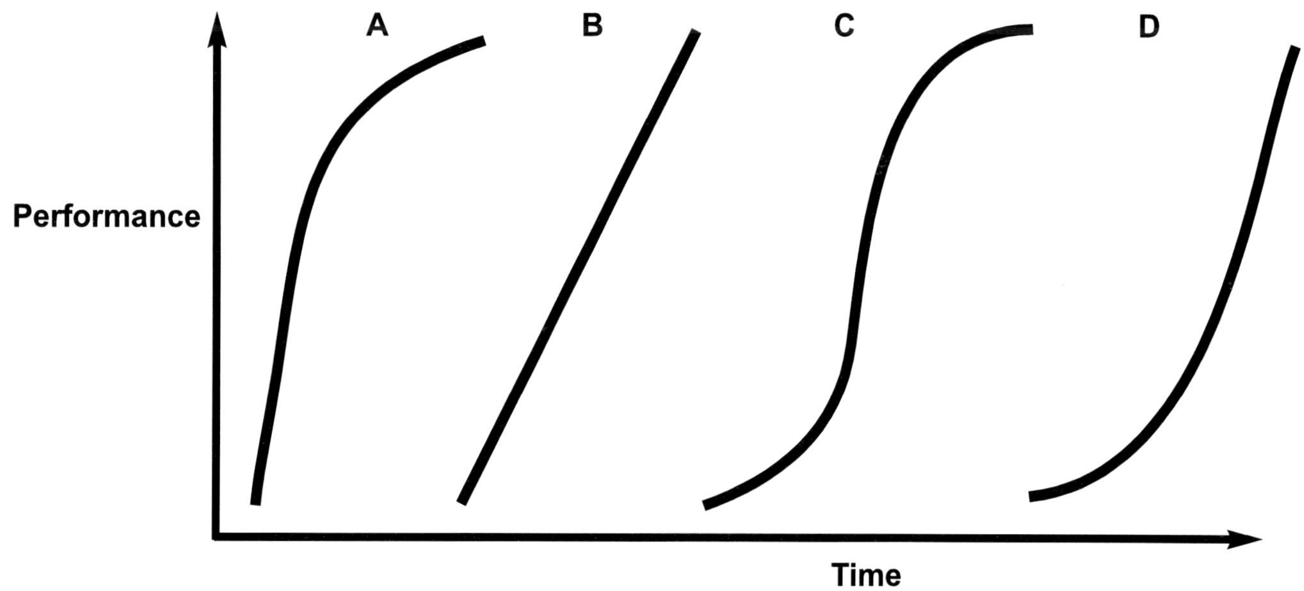

A steep curve indicates quick learning, a shallow curve indicates slower learning.

A A steep curve which becomes more shallow with time.

B A straight line, this indicates a constant and regular improvement in learning.

C An S shaped curve. Shallow, steep, then shallow.
Learning was relatively difficult at first then became more easy then became difficult again.

D A shallow curve which then steepens.
Learning was relatively hard at first then became easier.

Note: **Performance increase** may **not be** as a **result of learning**, but may have been due to **external factors** such as **luck** or **better weather**.
Or due to **physiological factors** such as:
- Better **recruitment** of muscle fibres.
- **Adaptations** to muscle tissue caused by long-term training.

Chapter 7 - PHASES OF MOVEMENT SKILL LEARNING

A BEGINNER'S LEARNING CURVE DURING ONE PRACTICE SESSION.

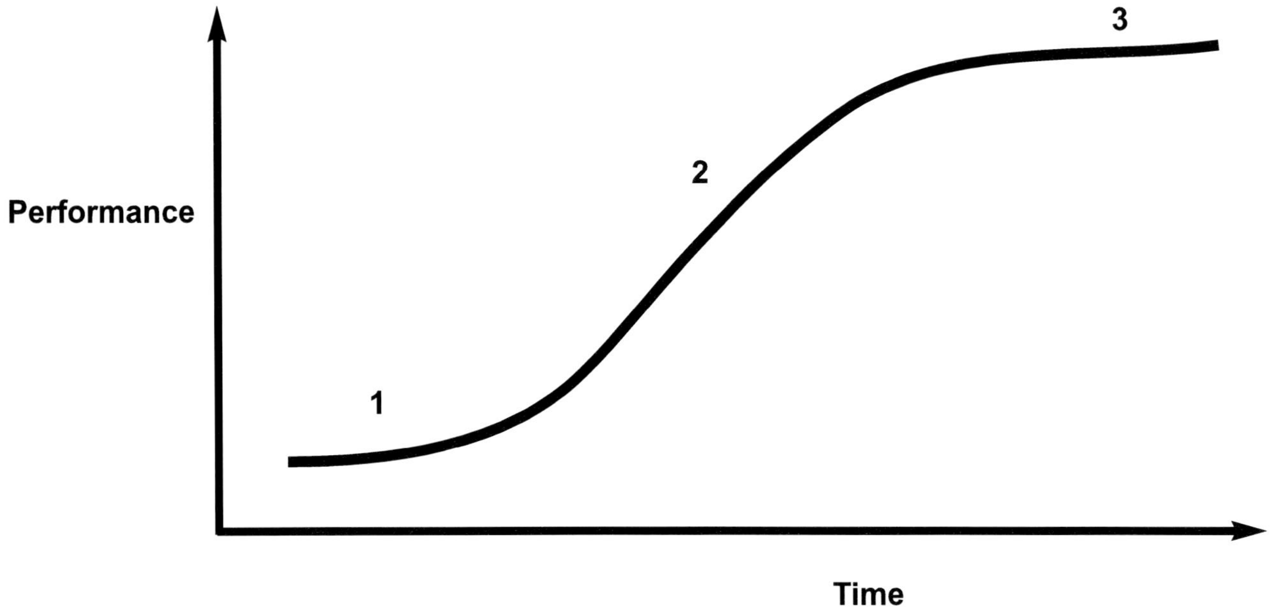

1. At first progress is **slow**.
The learner is still working out the **requirements** of the task.

2. When the learner **becomes aware** of what is required, performance improves greatly and he / she is free to practice.

3. At this point there is no change in performance (**plateau**).
This may be due to **lack of motivation** or the performer suffering from **fatigue**.

HOW TO AVOID PLATEAUX

- Do not attempt skill learning when **fatigued**.
- **Motivation** levels must be maintained.
- **Selective attention** is important, performers must concentrate on the **most important parts** of the skill.
- The performer must be **capable** of performing the skill.

Chapter 8 - TRANSFER OF LEARNING

Chapter 8 - TRANSFER OF LEARNING

TRANSFER OF LEARNING

Transfer of learning refers to the **effect that the learning of one skill has on the subsequent learning of other skills**.

POSITIVE TRANSFER

- The term **Positive Transfer** applies to situations in which **prior learning promotes present learning**.
- This means that the learning of task 1 has a beneficial effect on the learning of task 2. A tennis player could use prior learning when trying to learn the overhead serve in volleyball.
- The higher the degree of **similarity** between the parts of **two separate tasks** the greater the chance of positive transfer between the skills.

NEGATIVE TRANSFER

- The term **Negative Transfer** applies to situations in which **prior learning** has an **inhibiting** effect on **present learning**.
- The learning of task 1 has an adverse effect on the learning of task 2.
  For example, tennis players may find learning to play squash difficult:
    - Since tennis is played with a firm wrist.
    - To play squash you must learn to play with a flexible wrist action.
- **Negative transfer** is most likely to occur when a **new response** is required for an **old stimulus**.
  For example, a basketballer when playing netball:
    - May incur negative transfer when trying to respond to the new demands of netball using similar but inappropriate basketball skills.
    - If the stimulus is requiring the player to defend the ball carrier.
    - The old response would be to rush in and get within the three feet exclusion zone.
    - The appropriate new response would be to defend from the required
    - distance.
    - The basketball player will find this difficult.

  Another example, a rugby player:
    - Has always been taught to fall to the ground when tackled in order for his team mates to set up a ruck.
    - If the coach changes tactics and decides to play a mauling game.
    - It will be difficult for the player to stay standing in the tackle in order to set up a maul.
- **Negative transfer** effects are usually **temporary** and overcome with practice.

ZERO TRANSFER

- **Zero Transfer** implies that **prior learning** has **no effect** on **present learning**.
- The learning of task 1 has no effect on the learning of task 2.
  For example, football players would not be able to use their skills when learning to swim.

Chapter 8 - TRANSFER OF LEARNING

BILATERAL TRANSFER

- The notion of **bilateral transfer** states that **learning** can occur between **limbs**.
- A skill that is learned with one limb can affect the learning of the same skill with a different limb.
- Bilateral transfer is generally between arm and arm or leg to leg.
  For example, throwing with either hand and kicking with either foot.
- The **cognitive explanation**: **thinking about a skill** may improve transfer of that skill to an opposite limb.
- The **motor control explanation**: when learning a skill with the opposite limb, the performer does not have to start from scratch. A **schema** for the movement already exists for the **initial limb**. The schema has only to be **modified** for the new limb.

PROACTIVE TRANSFER

- **Proactive Transfer** describes the **effect** that **learning a skill** has on a skill that has **not yet been learned**. The effect could be **positive**, **negative** or **zero**.

RETROACTIVE TRANSFER

- **Retroactive Transfer** describes the effect that **learning a new skill** has **on** a **previously learned skill**. The effect could be **positive**, **negative** or **zero**.

Chapter 8 - TRANSFER OF LEARNING

STIMULUS AND RESPONSE GENERALISATION

- **Stimulus and response generalisation** are terms describing the **learning of generalised patterns of movement** rather than situation specific forms of movement.

- They are **forms of transfer** because the performer uses previously learned skills in new situations.

STIMULUS GENERALISATION

- According to **operant conditioning theory**, a particular **response** is **connected** to a particular **stimulus**.
  For example, a badminton student **always** plays an overhead clear to a shot played deep and high.

- **Stimulus generalisation** occurs when the **same response** is triggered by **anything resembling** the **original stimulus**.
  For example, the badminton student plays an overhead clear to any shot that arrives at above head height.

RESPONSE GENERALISATION

- **Response generalisation** theory suggests that once a response has been learned to a stimulus, a performer will react to the **same stimulus** by **responding** in a **number of similar but different ways**.

  For example, a cricket batter having learnt how to defend his / her stumps will learn how to play a number of different shots to the same type of delivery.

PROBLEMS ASSOCIATED WITH GENERALISATION

- With **stimulus generalisation**, a **player's** pattern of play becomes **predictable** and an opponent will find it easy to **anticipate**.

- **Response generalisation** does not give precision of movement.

- At high levels of sport it is important to be able to **differentiate** between **stimuli** and **respond to each stimulus specifically**.
  In our cricketer example, the cricket batter should play each delivery on its merit. This will require learning specific shots to play against specific deliveries. This could lead to **negative** transfer.

Chapter 8 - TRANSFER OF LEARNING

TEACHING TO INCREASE POSITIVE TRANSFER AND REDUCE NEGATIVE TRANSFER

Increase the similarity between the practice situation and game

- Transfer is said to be greatest between two tasks which are **similar**. **Practice** situations must closely match **competitive** situations (with opposition) if transfer is to be maximised.
  For example, basketball shooting against opposition. Introduce match day variables (different weather conditions, playing surfaces, opposition tactics, variation of crowd noise) into practice situations.

Make certain that the basics are fully learned

- The **basics** provide the **foundation** for any transfer of learning. Even experienced players should practise the basics and not be allowed to slip into bad habits.
- According to Magill "**maximising practice on the original task** is directly related to the likelihood of **positive transfer** to a subsequent task."

Increase the size and variability of the practice situation

- **Transfer of Learning** theory and **Schema Theory** both advocate the use of **varied practice** in order to provide a background from which **similar** but **different** movements can be planned.
- The sportsplayer is always faced with **different** and **new task situations**. The **experienced** player will be able to draw from **large generalised motor programmes**.
- It is important to **practise for every eventuality**, so, when faced with a new situation, the performer should be able to **transfer knowledge from a similar task**.
  For example, the cricket batter needs to learn how to face spin bowling and seam bowling on different pitches, and in different conditions.

Make the performer aware that transfer is possible

- Transfer of learning is only possible if the performer **realises** that he / she can transfer a previously learned skill to solve a new problem.
  For example, the teacher would allow for transfer by telling the pupil that the overhead serve in volleyball is very similar to the serve in tennis.

Make certain that the performer understands what is expected

- The performer needs to **understand** the **requirements of the task** so that he / she can get the task "ordered" in his / her mind. It is difficult to use transfer of learning if the performer has no idea of what needs to be achieved or how to achieve it.

Direct transfer of learning

- According to **Gestalt** theory **direct transfer of learning between one sport and another** can be best achieved by teaching the **principles** common to both. A number of **different skills** may have the same **underlying principle**.
  For example, positioning in team games. The games are different but the principle of not standing in line with a defender is the same for all games.
- Other principles for team games would include: support, keep possession, go forward, create space.

Chapter 8 - TRANSFER OF LEARNING

FACTORS AFFECTING THE AMOUNT OF TRANSFER OF LEARNING

Similarity between tasks

❒ You would expect a good racquet sports player to transfer striking skills to a batting game or to golf. Conversely a good swimmer would not have a lot of transfer to take to racquet sports.

Method of teaching

❒ A number of **different** teaching methods exist. Those which make use of **previously learnt similar skills** will enable the **greatest transfer** to take place.
For example, beating an opponent with a dribble in Hockey:
  - ❒ Teacher says "Hockey is like Football.
  - ❒ Imagine the ball is a football and the stick is your leg.
  - ❒ Try to fake the defender one way and you go the other.
  - ❒ Just like you would do in Football."

Bilateral transfer

❒ Transfer may well increase if a **similar skill** has been learnt with a different limb.
For example, learning to kick with your left foot would be more difficult if you could not already do it accurately and well with your right foot.

Level of initial learning

❒ It has already been stated that **foundations** need to have been laid to ensure further learning. Those who have been taught the **basic skills** will be in a better position to **transfer** those **skills** to more **advanced situations**. Consequently, learning correct skills at an early age is very important.

Complexity and organisation

❒ **Complexity** refers to the **number of component parts** to a skill. A skill is said to be complex when it has a large number of component parts. **Organisation** is concerned with the **interrelationships of the parts** of a skill.

❒ A skill that is **high in complexity** and **low in organisation** is best taught by making the performer practise related but **easier tasks first**, then setting harder tasks.
For example, dribbling a football around cones before trying to beat a player with a dribble.

❒ A skill that is **low in complexity** and **high in organisation** (it has a large timing element) is best taught by making the performer practise related but **harder tasks first**, then set easier tasks when the more difficult ones have been at least partially mastered.
For example, in shooting, make the target smaller at first.

Chapter 9 - TEACHING SKILLS IN PHYSICAL EDUCATION

Chapter 9 - TEACHING SKILLS IN PHYSICAL EDUCATION

PRESENTATION OF SKILLS

This section is concerned with the way a **teacher presents a skill to learners**. The teacher must decide whether to teach the entire skill or to break it down into parts and learn each part separately.

The decision on **which method is best** depends on a **number of factors** including:

- The **personality** of the learner.
- The **level of ability** of the performer.
- The **facilities** and **time** available.
- The **size** and **structure** of the **teaching group** (age, physique, gender).

Possible methods to present a skill include:

- **Whole** learning.
- **Part** learning.
- **Whole-part-whole** learning.
- **Progressive part** learning.

THE WHOLE METHOD

- The whole method involves teaching a skill in its entirety without breaking it down into parts.
- If at all possible, it is best to learn a skill using the whole method.

Advantages	Disadvantages
❒ The learner appreciates the end product.	❒ Unsuitable for complex skills.
❒ The learner gets a feeling of the timing of the movement.	❒ When the learner is at the early stage of learning he / she may not be able to cope with skills having high attentional demands.
❒ The learner can understand the relationship between the subroutines of the skill.	❒ For safety reasons skills may have to be broke down into parts.
❒ Learning is quicker because the learner does not have to learn how to put the parts together.	

Chapter 9 - TEACHING SKILLS IN PHYSICAL EDUCATION

THE PART METHOD

- This method involves breaking the skill into parts. Each part is practised separately and then the parts are joined together.

Advantages	Disadvantages
❐ Useful if the skill is complex as the learner can cope with small parts but not the whole.	❐ Transfer from part to whole may not be effective - it is difficult to split skills which are highly organised (the parts are linked together).
❐ It can be safer - the danger element can be reduced.	❐ Reduces kinaesthetic awareness.
❐ The method allows the teacher to focus on particular elements of the skill.	❐ The learner loses awareness of the end product.
❐ Learning in parts is motivating - it gives small steps of success.	❐ Continuity of the skill is lost.

WHOLE-PART-WHOLE METHOD

- At **first** the whole skill is attempted. If **errors** are apparent, then those parts of the skill which resulted in errors are practised in isolation before attempting the whole skill again.

PROGRESSIVE PART METHOD

- If a skill can be broken down into 5 parts, the parts are learned in the following order:
    - learn part 1,
    - learn part 2,
        - perform parts 1 and 2,
    - learn part 3,
        - perform parts 1,2 and 3,
    - learn part 4,
        - perform parts 1,2,3 and 4,
    - learn part 5,
        - perform parts 1,2,3,4 and 5.
- **Sequences** and **routines** are often learned in this way.

Chapter 9 - TEACHING SKILLS IN PHYSICAL EDUCATION

TASK COMPLEXITY AND TASK ORGANISATION

A knowledge of **task complexity** and **task organisation** will help the teacher to decide if a skill is best taught in the whole or part method.

Task Complexity

- If a skill is **high in complexity** it has a **large number of parts**.

Task Organisation

- This refers to the **relationship** between the **parts** of a skill.
- **Highly organised skills** have **parts** which are **closely linked** to each other.
- **Highly organised skills** have a **large timing component**.

- If a skill is **high in complexity** and **low in organisation** then practice in **parts** is recommended.

  For example, a single gymnastic move, a gym sequence or trampolining routine.
  - The whole skill has a large number of parts which are difficult to remember.
  - It will be easier for the learner if the skill is broken down.
  - Timing does not play a large part, so it does not matter if the skill is broken down.

- If a skill is **low in complexity** and **high in organisation** practice of the **whole** is recommended.

  For example, simple jumping, throwing, batting, hitting.
  - The skill is relatively simple, so does not need to be broken down.
  - High in organisation means that the timing of the skill is paramount.
  - Timing can only be improved if the skill is practised as a whole.

Chapter 9 - TEACHING SKILLS IN PHYSICAL EDUCATION

PRACTICE CONDITIONS

This section is concerned with the way in which a skill is best practised. It may be best to practise for a repeated number of short sessions or it may be best to practise for long periods until the skill is learned.

FIXED PRACTICE (set drills)

- This method is used primarily for **closed skill practice** but can be used to improve open skills. The learner practises a set task without any change.
  For example, a gym / trampolining / diving routine, a throw or jump, a set practice or skill in a game (free kick, service reception).

VARIABLE PRACTICE

- The learner practises the **same task** in a number of **different** ways.
  For example, in an invasion game, a player practises shooting from different angles and distances.
  This method helps to improve the schema for shooting of the player.

MASSED v DISTRIBUTED PRACTICE

Should the learner practise **continually for long spells** (**massed**) or should the learner **spread practice out** in order to practise for **short periods of time regularly** (**distributed**)?

- The learner needs to be engaged in a practice method that allows him / her to try hard and **concentrate** fully. Consequently, the best method depends on the learner, but as a rule it is agreed that **distributed practice is most effective**.

Massed is best:

- When the performer is **highly motivated** and can cope with **long** practice sessions.
- When the task is **simple** and can be fully learned in one session.
- In the **later stages of learning** when the elite performer can cope with long practice sessions.
- In the **early stages of learning** when, through **trial and error,** the novice performer is able to stumble across the correct response.

Distributed is best:

- In the **early stages of learning** when the novice performer may get easily bored or **fatigued**.
- When the **energy demands** are high.
- When the task is **complex** and will require a number of practice sessions.
- When **motivation is low** or when the task is boring.

Chapter 9 - TEACHING SKILLS IN PHYSICAL EDUCATION

MENTAL PRACTICE / MENTAL REHEARSAL

Definition: practice or rehearsal of a skill **without** actual physical **movement**.

Used by: skiers, golfers, athletes, tennis players, and gymnasts.

How: **watching a demonstration** or film, reading or listening to instructions, imagining movements.

HOW DOES IT WORK?

THE NEUROMUSCULAR EXPLANATION

❒ **Thinking about a movement** which actually **produces nerve impulses** that fire in the correct order. Consequently, mental practice is supposed to **result** in **actual physical practice**.

❒ There is little evidence to support this explanation but it could be helpful in improving the quality of kinaesthetic feedback.

THE COGNITIVE EXPLANATION

❒ **Thinking about strategies and tactics** can help the performer make the correct decisions on the field. It is supposed to help the performer anticipate. In this way the performer is better able to **understand** skills and tactics.

THE CONFIDENCE EXPLANATION

❒ Mental rehearsal has been claimed to **improve the confidence** of performers, which should lead to **improved motivation** and performance. Mental rehearsal also **readies the performer for action** and **stimulates** both **mental and physical faculties**. It is like a mental warm up.

USES

❒ Used in a **potentially dangerous** situation as a safe way of practising.
❒ Used to **improve the confidence** of performers who have low confidence.
❒ Performers can re-enact past events and **practise preferred outcomes**.
❒ Used to help **focus** the mind, as the performer is able to imagine perfect performance without harmful distractions.
❒ The performer can practise to achieve the **preferred state of arousal** for his / her sport.
❒ Used during **injury** or periods of **rehabilitation** to **maintain neuromuscular** pathways.

Chapter 9 - TEACHING SKILLS IN PHYSICAL EDUCATION

GUIDANCE METHODS

This section is concerned with the methods the coach uses to **communicate** the important elements of a skill.

The **3 methods of communication** a teacher may use are:

- **Verbal**: the **learner is told** what to do.
- **Manual**: the **learner's limbs are physically manipulated** into the correct position.
- **Visual**: the **learner is shown** what to do.

  - Probably not all forms of guidance are of equal significance to the learner. Some people are **more receptive** to verbal guidance and others to visual guidance.
  - Different forms of guidance are more or less meaningful at different **stages of learning**.

VERBAL GUIDANCE

- **Verbal guidance** can be from the teacher or by the learner to him / herself.
- **Verbal instructions** should be kept to a **minimum** during the early **stages of learning** due to the novice's limited capacity to process information. **Instructions** should be **brief** and to the point.
- The teacher should leave a **gap** between the end of performance and the onset of verbal guidance. This gives the learner **time to process** any **intrinsic feedback**.
- **Self-verbalisation** can be used to improve performance.
- Verbal guidance is useful at **later stages of learning** when the elite performer has a **greater capacity** to **attend to information**.
- Ultimately the learner must perform on his / her own. As learning progresses, verbal instruction should be interspersed with greater practice periods.

Chapter 9 - TEACHING SKILLS IN PHYSICAL EDUCATION

MANUAL GUIDANCE

Manual guidance can take 2 forms:

- If an activity is potentially **hazardous**, **equipment** can be used to prevent the learner making incorrect movements.
  For example, a somersaulting rig for trampolining.
  This form of guidance is known as **mechanical guidance**.

- At the early stage of learning (especially for the young) the teacher may need to **correctly position the limbs** of the learner.
  For example, a coach will guide the limbs and trunk into the correct body position for a golf swing.

- Manual guidance is useful because it can give the performer the **confidence** and physical support necessary to perform skills **correctly** and **safely**. It can be **problematic** when the performer becomes too **reliant** on mechanical guidance. Guidance also **restricts** the performers own **kinaesthesis** because the performer is unaware of how the movement should feel unaided.

VISUAL GUIDANCE

- This method is useful at every stage of learning but especially useful for the **beginner** who needs to gain a **mental picture of correct performance**.

- **Demonstrations** at the **early stage** of learning **should be at full speed** to enable the beginner to gain an idea of the **correct sequencing** or timing of the movement.

- At **later stages of learning demonstrations** can be **slowed down** to highlight points of detail.

- **Demonstrations** must show a good technical model to enable the **learner** to attempt **to reproduce** the desired skills.

Chapter 9 - TEACHING SKILLS IN PHYSICAL EDUCATION

TEACHING STYLES

According to **Mosston's spectrum of teaching styles**, the way a pupil is taught ranges between two extremes:

- At one end of the spectrum the learner is told what to do and how to do it.
- At the other end of the spectrum, the learner solves problems him / herself, working out what to do and how to do it.

THE COMMAND STYLE

- In this style, the **teacher** makes all the **major decisions**. The **learner** is only required to **follow instructions**. The **learner** does **not make any decisions**. **Conforming behaviour** is the result of this style of teaching; all **learners** should respond in the **same way**.
  For example, teaching the forward roll in gymnastics. Teacher's commands:
  - Starting position, hands flat on the floor.
  - Tuck head in, push and kick.
  - Rounded back, land on shoulders.
  - Push and stand up, finishing position.

Advantages	Disadvantages
❐ Pupils learn skills very quickly.	❐ All the thinking is taken away from the learner so the learner will not know how to react in a new situation.
❐ Ensures safety for potentially dangerous skills (for example, javelin).	❐ The method does not fully stimulate or challenge every pupil.
❐ Easy for the teacher to gauge the standard of performance as everyone is doing the same task.	❐ The method does not cater for different abilities within one group.

THE PRACTICE STYLE

- The **teacher sets the task** then the **pupils go away and do it**.
  For example, in a hockey practice, 2v1, the teacher commands:
  - Draw the defender and pass, do it five times then swap positions.

THE RECIPROCAL STYLE

- This involves the learners **working in pairs**. One is the **doer** the other is the **observer / coach**. The **task is set by the teacher** and the points of correct technique / tactics are given to the observer by the teacher. The **doer practises the technique**. The **observer** watches and **gives feedback** related to the information given by the teacher

Advantages	Disadvantages
❐ Improves personal and social skills.	❐ The learner may not be giving the doer correct feedback.
❐ Develops evaluative and performance skills.	
❐ Learners feel more in control of their actions and are liable to be more motivated.	

Chapter 9 - TEACHING SKILLS IN PHYSICAL EDUCATION

TEACHING STYLES (continued)

THE SELF-CHECK STYLE

❐ Learners **work individually** on **tasks set by the teacher**. **The teacher** gives **correct techniques** to the learner (usually on paper to allow for constant checking and rechecking). The **learner performs the task** and **compares** the **result** with an **ideal performance**.

THE INCLUSION STYLE

❐ This style allows for the idea that the **ability range** within a group may be **large**. Consequently, **tasks** will need to be set which will **stimulate** and **challenge all** pupils.
For example, the teacher chooses an easy form of the task for some, and a hard form of the same task for others. In shooting, learners decide how far from the goal to shoot (10m, 20m, or 30m).

THE GUIDED DISCOVERY STYLE

❐ The **teacher sets a problem** and **leads** the **pupil** to the "correct" **answer**.
For example, in cricket, what stroke should you play to a short-pitched delivery outside leg stump (a ball bouncing high and wide of the stumps)?
The teacher is looking for the learner to play the pull or hook shot. The teacher tries to get the answer by asking:
  - ❐ Do you play with a straight or horizontal bat?
  - ❐ How do you get the power?
  - ❐ How do you keep the ball down?

Advantages	Disadvantages
❐ The learner develops an ability to solve problems. Consequently, when faced with a new problem he / she has the ability to solve it. ❐ It stimulates the learner mentally and physically. ❐ The learner becomes more independent and ceases to look to the teacher for answers. ❐ The learner should be fully challenged and well motivated. ❐ It can lead to transfer of learning when the learner discovers similarities between skills and games.	❐ The method can be time consuming and slower than command style. ❐ It is difficult to teach for "text book" performance since learners find their own answers, which may be close to but not quite the same as "text book".

THE PROBLEM SOLVING STYLE

❐ The **teacher sets the problem** and the **learner finds the answer**. Learners are not guided towards a "correct" answer but simply helped to find an answer.
For example,
  - ❐ In gymnastics, find a balance on one foot and one hand.
  - ❐ In basketball, 1v1, find a way of dribbling past your opponent.

Section 2 - Sport Psychology

Section 2 - Sport Psychology

Chapter 10 - INDIVIDUAL ASPECTS OF SPORT PERFORMANCE - PERSONALITY

Chapter 10 - INDIVIDUAL ASPECTS OF SPORT PERFORMANCE - PERSONALITY

PERSONALITY

Personality has been defined as the **sum total** of an **individual's characteristics** which makes him / her unique. **Personality characteristics** could be things such as being shy, tense, relaxed, sensitive, aggressive, outgoing.

- **Personality** is relevant to sport performance because certain personality characteristics can be said to aid performance.
  For example, drive, determination, competitiveness.

HOW ARE PERSONALITIES FORMED?

This next section will examine three groups of theories which explain the formation of personality.

- **Trait Theory**, which explains personality as being **hereditary** and determined at birth depending on the characteristics inherited by a child from its parents.
- **Social Learning Theory**, which explains personality as being caused by a number of **environmental influences**. The theory states that personality is **learned**.
- **Interactionist Theory**, which explains personality as a function of **hereditary and situational** factors. This theory says that personality is **inherited and learned**.

TRAIT THEORY (Eysenck, Cattell)

According to trait theorists:

- People **cannot help** the way they act because personality is **determined at birth**. Everyone is born with a number of **personality traits**. A **trait** is an **underlying and enduring** (relatively long lasting and permanent) **tendency to behave** in a certain way.
- Cattell identified 171 traits. We all have a number of traits in varying degrees of intensity.
- Personality **does not change over time** and the **situation has little effect** on personality.
- **Traits are arranged in a hierarchy** with the strongest at the top and the weakest at the bottom. We are most likely to display our strong traits and less likely to display our weakest traits.

Example of a hierarchical organisation of traits:

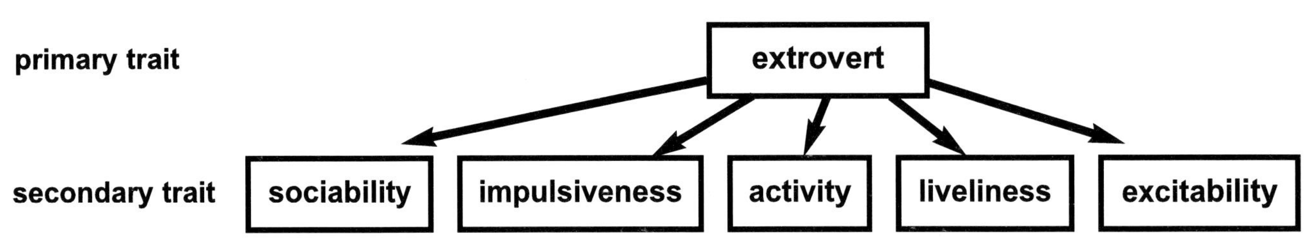

Chapter 10 - INDIVIDUAL ASPECTS OF SPORT PERFORMANCE - PERSONALITY

EYSENCK'S TRAIT THEORY (1968)

According to Eysenck the **trait** that is **most likely to be displayed** is known as the **personality type**. Below the personality type (in the hierarchy) is a group of **strong traits** known as **personality traits**. Below the personality traits there are a group of **weaker traits** called **general habits**.

- Eysenck arranged personality along 2 dimensions:
  - **Introversion - Extroversion**.
  - **Stable - Unstable (stability)**.
- A person could be a **stable extrovert**, **stable introvert**, **unstable extrovert**, **unstable introvert** or anywhere in between.
- Later a third dimension was added, **Psychotic - Non-psychotic (psychotism)**.

EYSENCK'S PERSONALITY DIMENSIONS

UNSTABLE

Unstable - Introverted	Unstable - Extroverted
moody	**touchy**
anxious	**restless**
rigid	**aggressive**
sober	**excitable**
pessimistic	**changeable**
reserved	**impulsive**
unsociable	**optimistic**
quiet	**active**

INTROVERTED **EXTROVERTED**

Stable - Introverted	Stable - Extroverted
passive	**sociable**
careful	**outgoing**
thoughtful	**talkative**
peaceful	**responsive**
controlled	**easy going**
reliable	**lively**
even tempered	**carefree**
calm	**leadership**

STABLE

- According to Eysenck, a person could be located anywhere along the two dimensions.
- **Introverts** are: **passive**, **quiet** and **unsociable**.
- **Extroverts** are: **sociable**, **outgoing** and **active**.
- **Emotional stability** is characterised by being: **calm**, **even tempered**, **carefree**.
  Emotional instability is characterised by being: **moody**, **anxious**, **rigid**.
- **Introverts** are **more easily aroused** than extroverts. **Introverts** are more likely to **obey rules**, are liable to be **more restrained** and **prefer working alone**. **Extroverts** prefer **working in groups**.

Chapter 10 - INDIVIDUAL ASPECTS OF SPORT PERFORMANCE - PERSONALITY

CATTELL'S TRAIT THEORY (1965)

According to Cattell, a **hierarchy of personality traits** exists with **source traits** at the **top**. These are **behaviours** which **do not vary** and are **most likely to be displayed**. On a **lower level** are **surface traits** which are **groups of behaviour** which are displayed with **varying levels of intensity and regularity**.

- Cattell identified **16 primary traits** and developed the **Cattell 16 PF questionnaire** to measure them.
- The 16 primary traits are:
  sociability
  general ability
  ego strength
  dominance
  surgency
  conscientiousness
  adventurousness
  sensitiveness
  pretension
  bohemianism
  shrewdness
  insecurity
  radicalism
  self-sufficiency
  will-power
  tenseness.

TYPE A AND TYPE B PERSONALITIES

- This theory examines personality and how people cope with stress. It divides people into two categories: **Type A** and **Type B**. This theory has also been termed as **The Narrow Band Approach** (Girdano et al 1990).
- **Type A personalities tend to**:
  - Have a **strong desire to succeed**.
  - Exhibit high levels of **alertness** and are **easily aroused**.
  - Work at a **fast pace**.
  - Find it **hard to delegate**.
  - Need to be **in control**.
  - Experience **high levels of stress**.
- **Type B personalities tend to**:
  - Be more **relaxed**.
  - **Delegate** easily.
  - Be **less competitive**.
  - Be **tolerant**.
  - **Allow time** for jobs to be completed.
  - Experience **low levels of stress**.
- **Both** personality types can be **effective** in **different situations**.

Chapter 10 - INDIVIDUAL ASPECTS OF SPORT PERFORMANCE - PERSONALITY

SOCIAL LEARNING THEORY

The major theorist was **Bandura** (1977). The main points of the theory are:

- People **behave differently** in **different situations**.
- Personality is **learned**.
- Personality is learned through:
  Socialisation
  Observational Learning
  Modelling
  Vicarious Conditioning.

- **Social learning theory** overcame some of the **limitations of trait theory**. Elements of **Trait Theory** for which **there is no evidence** are:
  - Traits can be identified, are stable and enduring.
  - The personality type of athletes is different from that of non-athletes.
  - Certain personality types are better suited for particular sports.
  - Situation does not play a major role in personality formation.

- The main **difference** between trait theory and social learning theory is **the importance of the environment**. **Social learning theory** states that the **response to a stimulus cannot be predicted**, people can consciously **change their response** depending on the **situation**.

- For example, if a person were punched, **trait theorists** would say that a person with high trait aggression would always punch back. **Social learning theorists** would argue that the response would depend on the situation (how hard he was hit, by whom, in what environment, what choices he had).

MAJOR CONCEPTS

Observational Learning

- **Observational Learning** is the **learning** of behaviours simply by **watching others**. The **people who are observed** are known as **Models**.

Modelling

- The **process** of observational learning is also known as **Modelling**.
  For example, a novice tennis player could learn how to play a forehand top spin drive simply by watching a model. He / she could also learn how to abuse the umpire by watching other players.

Vicarious Conditioning

- **Vicarious Conditioning** is the **learning of emotional responses** through observational learning.
  For example, if an elite tennis player gets angry at a call that goes against her, a young player watching this could learn the need to become angry in the same situation (even though it would be better to accept the call and concentrate on playing the game).

Socialisation

- The **greatest amount of learning** takes place at an **early age** through **socialisation**. **Socialisation** is the **process** by which **society trains its children** to behave like adults. Through socialisation we learn the correct patterns of behaviour (**norms**), what is right and wrong (**values**), and our **status** and **role** in society.

- Physical education and **sport** can act as **part** of the **socialisation process**. PE and sport help to transmit the **norms and values of society**. Sport is seen as developing values such as **fair play, tolerance, cooperation, teamwork** and **determination**.

Chapter 10 - INDIVIDUAL ASPECTS OF SPORT PERFORMANCE - PERSONALITY

BANDURA'S MODEL OF OBSERVATIONAL LEARNING (1977)

The model has **4 stages**:

- **Attention Processes** — **what to look for** in the model's performance.
- **Retention Processes** — **how to remember** the model's performance.
- **Motor Reproduction** — **how to copy** the model's performance.
- **Motivational Processes** — the **reasons why** a person would want to copy the model's performance.

How to Improve Observational Learning:

Attention	Because the **learner** has **limited attentional capacity** he / she will need to use **selective attention** to pick out the **relevant cues**. A teacher will need to highlight these cues.
Retention	**Repeated demonstrations** will help retention, as will **mental rehearsal**.
Motor Reproduction	The learner's performance can be improved with **practice** and through the use of **intrinsic and extrinsic feedback**.
Motivation	The learner must first **want to copy** the model's performance, he / she must have a **reason**. The **status of the model** and the **importance of the task** will affect motivation.

- Whether or not a person **decides to copy** the performance of a model depends on a number of factors. Modelling behaviour is likely if:
    - The **model** is perceived as having **high status**. **Models** which command **power** or **respect** are **more likely to be copied**.
    - The **model's behaviour** is perceived as being **relevant** to the subject. For example, copying the behaviour of a player who plays in the same position as the subject.
    - The model is of a similar **age** or **sex**.
    - The model's behaviour is **reinforced**.
      A person seeing **behaviour rewarded** is **more likely to copy** that behaviour. Similarly, if the **learner's behaviour is rewarded** then that behaviour is **more likely to be repeated**.

Chapter 10 - INDIVIDUAL ASPECTS OF SPORT PERFORMANCE - PERSONALITY

INTERACTIONIST THEORY

❐ According to **Interactionist Theory**, **behaviour** (**B**) is a **function** (**f**) of **personality** traits (**P**) and **environmental conditions** (**E**).

B = f (P,E).

❐ In other words, **Interactionist Theory** is a **combination** of the best bits of **Trait Theory** and **Social Learning Theory**.

PERSONALITY TESTS AND PERSONALITY PROFILING

❐ Personality research has been used to answer questions such as:
- ❐ Is there such a thing as an **athletic personality**?
- ❐ Do athletes from **different sports** exhibit **different personality** characteristics?

❐ If athletes' personalities **differ** from those of non-athletes then coaches could select young athletes on the basis of personality as well as ability. Coaches could also try to alter the personality of athletes to better reflect the desired personality type.

❐ The first thing a coach would need to do is assess or measure the personality of different athletes.

PERSONALITY MEASUREMENT

❐ Personality has been assessed in a number of ways including:
- ❐ **Observations of performance**.
- ❐ **Interviews**.
- ❐ **Personality inventories** (**questionnaires**).

❐ A few of the more well-known personality tests or profiles are set out below.

THE MINNESOTA MULTIPHASIC PERSONALITY INVENTORY (MMPI)

❐ This inventory contains 550 items or statements which the subject decides are **true or false** in relation to him / herself. The strength of feeling is found using a scale. The MMPI was designed to be used by trained psychologists and is **not a sport specific test**.

THE EYSENCK PERSONALITY INVENTORY (EPI)

❐ This inventory measures **two dimensions**: **Neuroticism-Stability** and **Introversion-Extroversion**.
- ❐ **Neuroticism** refers to general **emotional stability** and an individual's predisposition to **neurotic breakdown under stress**.
- ❐ **Extroversion** refers to **uninhibited**, **outgoing**, **impulsive** and **social inclinations** of a person.

❐ Each of the two dimensions is measured by a "yes" or "no" response to 24 questions.

Chapter 10 - INDIVIDUAL ASPECTS OF SPORT PERFORMANCE - PERSONALITY

CATTELL 16 P.F. QUESTIONNAIRE

- This questionnaire looks at the **16 Primary factors** or primary traits identified by Cattell. The questionnaire is in the form of 187 statements to which the subject responds "yes", "occasionally" or "no". The test gives a score for each of the primary personality factors.

The next two tests specifically measure personalities thought to be important for sports performers.

TUTKO ATHLETIC MOTIVATION INVENTORY

- This involves a questionnaire attempting to measure levels of particular personality characteristics thought valuable for sports performers (**drive**, **determination**, **leadership**, **aggression**, and **self-confidence**).

MORGAN (1977) PROFILE OF MOOD STATES (POMS)

- Morgan measured the mood states of **tension**, **depression**, **anger**, **vigour**, **fatigue** and **confusion**.
- When results from all the mood states were combined, Morgan found that the **profile of athletes** was **different** from that of **non-athletes**.
- The phrase "**iceberg profile**" was used to describe the profile of **athletes**. This is because the score for certain moods (**anger** and **vigour**) appeared **higher** than the norm, whilst the majority of mood scores were below the norm.

Chapter 10 - INDIVIDUAL ASPECTS OF SPORT PERFORMANCE - PERSONALITY

LIMITATIONS OF PERSONALITY TESTS AND PERSONALITY PROFILES

The idea that **certain personalities** or moods lead to **sporting success** has **not been proven**. In general it can be said that **personality measurement** has **not been able** to predict **success at sport** for the following reasons:

- **Not all athletes** exhibit the traits of the "**iceberg profile**".
- **Sporting success** may lead to a **change in personality** rather than vice versa.
- **POMS** is a measure of **mood**, not personality. It should be used carefully as **mood** can **change** significantly over time.
- **Self-report questionnaires** may **lack accuracy** for a number of reasons:
    - Subjects may respond in the way they believe they **ought to respond** rather than respond by recording how they actually feel.
    - Subjects' answers may be **affected by their mood** or by their thoughts about the test or tester.
- **Not all tests** have produced **repeatable** results, calling the test into question:
    - Many studies were done without a good reason.
    - Personality studies were often not carefully thought out and designed.
    - Researchers often used any test they could without knowing why.
    - The experimental procedure and analysis were not rigorous enough.
- Researchers have often tested using **inappropriate subjects**, **small numbers** of subjects, or have used **inappropriate tests**.
  For example, **MMPI** which is a **clinical psychiatric test**, not a sports science test.
- Many researchers have tried to make too much of their findings, they have over-generalised or have **attributed an effect as a cause**.
  For example, volleyball players have been found to be more independent than non-volleyball players. Therefore to be a volleyball player a person should be independent. This is not true: effect is being confused with cause.

Researchers have offered the following summary of **conclusions about the personality of sports performers**, summarised by:

- **Successful athletes** display **drive**, **determination**, **leadership** and **self-confidence** (Ogilvie).
- **Successful athletes** have a more **positive outlook** (Morgan).
- Sport can **affect** personality. The demands of a sport dictate particular responses.
    - For example, rugby players need to be aggressive.
    - Golfers need to be calm under pressure (Saunders).
- **Sports people** tend to show traits of **extroversion**, **enthusiasm** and **aggression** (Butt).
- People in **team sports** are more **extrovert** than those playing individual sports (Davis).

Chapter 11 - INDIVIDUAL ASPECTS OF SPORT PERFORMANCE - AGGRESSION

Chapter 11 - INDIVIDUAL ASPECTS OF SPORT PERFORMANCE - AGGRESSION

AGGRESSION

According to Dolard (1939) "**aggression is a response having for its goal the injury of a human being**".

- **Aggression** must be directed against something that is living and it must have the **intention of causing it injury or harm**.

- **Violence** is a severe form of aggression.

- **Instrumental aggression** is aggression **occurring in the achievement of a non-aggressive goal**.
  For example, boxing, in which the punching of an opponent (above the waist) is allowed within the rules as a means of winning a contest.
  Or rugby, attacking the other team's best player with valid but hard tackles (within the rules) in order to intimidate the player and have more chance of winning.
  Instrumental aggression is sometimes called **channelled aggression**.

- **Reactive aggression** is the **aggressive response** to **other aggressive behaviour**.
  For example, getting involved in football hooliganism.

- **Instrumental aggression** is a means to an end, the end being winning. In comparison, **reactive aggression** has only one end, **harming** opponents or their representatives.

AGGRESSION VERSES ASSERTION

- The table below tries to outline the **difference** between **aggression** and **assertion**, although at times the distinction can be a little blurred as strong assertive play can often be interpreted as being aggressive.

Aggression	Assertion
❒ Behaviour intended to cause harm.	❒ Behaviour directed towards a non-violent goal.
❒ Behaviour outside the rules.	❒ Behaviour is within the rules.
❒ Always involves the use of force.	❒ Can involve the use of force.
❒ Uncontrolled.	❒ Channelled / controlled.
❒ Hostile.	❒ Instrumental.

Chapter 11 - INDIVIDUAL ASPECTS OF SPORT PERFORMANCE - AGGRESSION

CAUSES OF AGGRESSION

It is difficult to accurately identify the cause of any aggressive act in sport but contributory factors can be identified.

Arousal

Increased arousal can bring about **aggression**.

- Heightened arousal levels bring about the **fight-or-flight response**, readying the body for aggression.
- **Threatening situations** can often cause increased arousal. The **threat** could be a **physical** one, it could be caused by **pain** or the **fear of getting hurt**. The threat could be a **threat to the ego**, the fear of losing, or even the fear of looking a fool.
- Often players decide to "get their retaliation in first".

Frustration

Frustration at not being able to achieve an individual or team goal can lead to aggression.

- This could be **caused** by other players, officials, spectators or even playing badly. The effect could be heightened when **playing away** from home.

League Position

- Studies have shown that the most aggressive teams are those at the **top** and **bottom** of league tables. Teams fighting for honours or fighting to avoid relegation.

Stage of Moral Reasoning

According to **Bredemeier** (1983), on the journey from childhood to adulthood a person passes through a number of **stages of moral reasoning**.

- The young child may reason that there is nothing wrong with aggression as it is an effective means of getting his / her own way. An **adult may reason** that violence in sport is **morally wrong**.
- Bredemeier argues that aggression can occur when a person **gets stuck at an early stage of moral reasoning development**, believing that aggression can be justified.
- **Bracketed morality** occurs when, for example, the moral rules for contact sports are different to those of society in general.

Chapter 11 - INDIVIDUAL ASPECTS OF SPORT PERFORMANCE - AGGRESSION

THEORIES OF AGGRESSION

There are four main theories which attempt to explain aggression:

❐ **Instinct Theory**	Aggression is innate.
❐ **Frustration-Aggression Theory**	Aggression is a drive derived from frustration. Frustration is caused by the non-achievement of a goal.
❐ **Aggressive-Cue Hypothesis**	Aggression is a learned response to frustrating situations.
❐ **Social Learning Theory**	Aggression is learned.

INSTINCT THEORY

❐ This theory states that **aggression** is **innate**. We are all born with a certain **predisposition to be aggressive**.

❐ **Aggressive tendencies** are **difficult** to **control**.

❐ Instinct theory has likened the build up of aggression to the build up of rain in a rainbutt. The **stress of everyday life** builds up the **aggression inside** of us. Eventually the aggression will be let out, often in a big outburst of violent or deviant behaviour.

❐ **Sport** acts as a **cathartic release**, purging all aggressive tendencies. Instinct theorists see **aggression in sport** as being **healthy**. Within **sport**, **aggression** is **controlled**. If sport were not available aggression would be let out in more dangerous ways.

PROBLEMS WITH INSTINCT THEORY

❐ There is **little substantial evidence** that this theory describes the reasons for aggressive behaviour.

❐ The theory does **not consider** the importance of **environmental** and **situational** factors.

❐ It assumes sport **allows** people to be aggressive. But the **rules** of many sports make it difficult to be aggressive.

❐ It assumes that **playing sport** can lead to a **more peaceful society**. Yet some of the largest sporting nations are also the same nations that are waging war.

Chapter 11 - INDIVIDUAL ASPECTS OF SPORT PERFORMANCE - AGGRESSION

FRUSTRATION-AGGRESSION THEORY - DOLLARD (1939)

- This theory states that **aggression** is the result of **frustrating circumstances**. If people are frustrated in being unable to achieve a goal they can respond aggressively.

- The theory highlights the fact that **sport is frustrating** in itself, since one player is always trying to prevent the other from winning, hence the other player's goals are frustrated. As a consequence it is **sport itself** that can **cause aggression**.

- This theory is sometimes known as **drive theory** because **frustration** leads to an **uncontrollable drive** to be **aggressive**. The **aggression** is usually **directed against** the **cause of frustration** but can be directed elsewhere.
  For example, the player who is frustrated by the referee could be aggressive to an opposition player because the degree of punishment would be less severe.

- **Coaches** should therefore help performers cope with frustrating circumstances by trying to make them **channel their aggression** towards a team or individual **goal**, and turn reactive aggression into instrumental aggression.
  For example, the rugby player could ruck or tackle harder.

- In sports where any form of **aggression is forbidden**, the coach could try to make the player **release** his / her need for **aggression in a different way**.
  For example, a tennis player's cathartic release could be obtained by shouting, but care needs to be taken, since in some sports even shouting is seen to be inappropriate and against the rules.

- This theory indicates that **aggression** will cause an **unwanted switch of attention** from the player's main focus of the game. The coach's main **aim** should be to try to **regain** the player's **attentional focus**.

- The main problem with **frustration-aggression theory** is that it does **not explain** why people are **not aggressive** when the situation is frustrating.

Chapter 11 - INDIVIDUAL ASPECTS OF SPORT PERFORMANCE - AGGRESSION

AGGRESSIVE-CUE HYPOTHESIS

- The **aggressive-cue hypothesis** attempts to explain aggression by reformulating the **frustration-aggression** theory and **combining** it with **social learning theory**.

- **Berkowitz** (1973) argued that **frustration-aggression theory** was **flawed** because frustration does not always lead to aggression. **Aggression** only **results** from frustration **if an aggressive response was appropriate**.

- In other words an aggressive act is a **learned response** to a frustrating situation. For example, fighting in Australian Rules Football and Ice Hockey. Aggression is viewed in these sports as an appropriate response to frustration. But a cricketer attacking the bowler who has just caught him / her out would be highly inappropriate.

Diagramatic Representation of the Aggressive-Cue Hypothesis

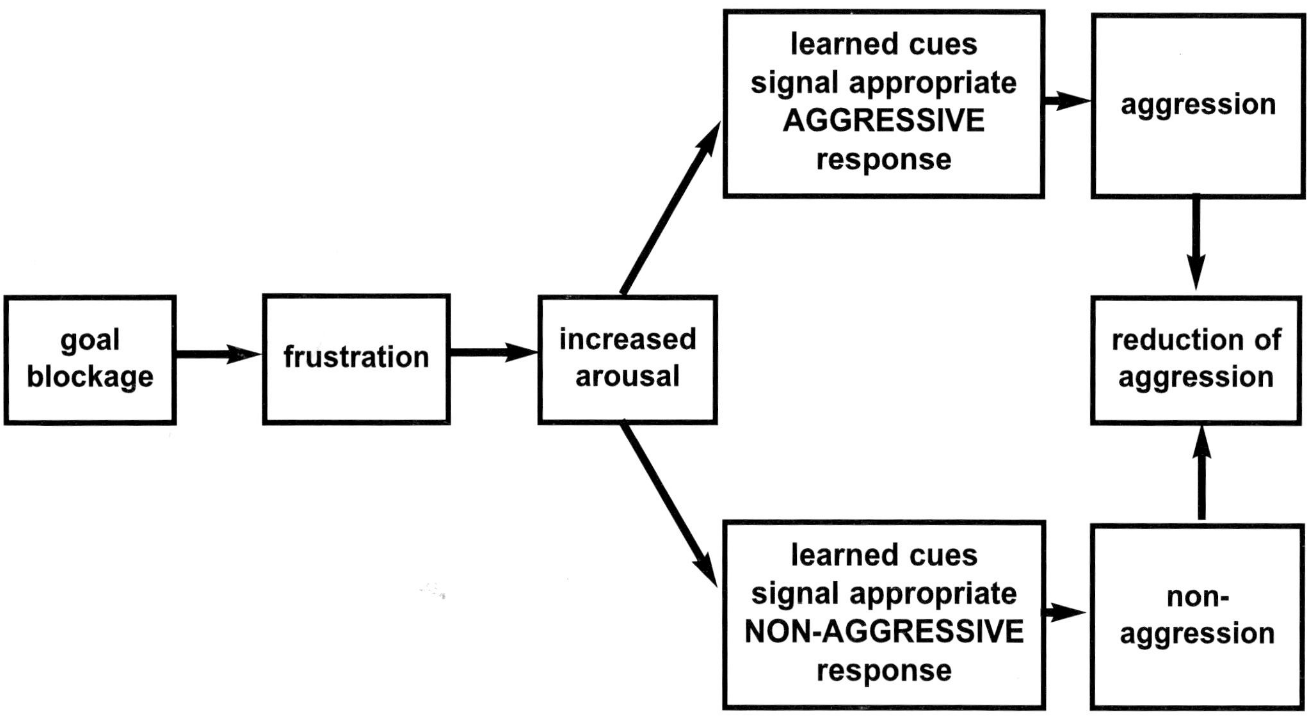

Chapter 11 - INDIVIDUAL ASPECTS OF SPORT PERFORMANCE - AGGRESSION

SOCIAL LEARNING THEORY

- **Social Learning Theory** says that **aggression is learned**.
- Aggression is learned through the **primary socialising agents**:
  - **Parents**.
  - **Teachers**.
  - **Friends**.
- A person can **learn an aggressive act** either by being **taught** it, or through **observational learning** and **modelling**.
- **Sport** can **promote** both **aggressive** and **non-aggressive** acts.
- If a **learner** (novice) **observes** a **role model** perform an aggressive act, it is likely that he / she will want to **copy** it. Conversely, if a learner observes a role model perform a non-aggressive act it is likely that he / she will want to copy it.
- If a **learner** is **rewarded** for an aggressive act it is likely he / she will want to **repeat** it. On the other hand, if a learner is rewarded for a non-aggressive act it is likely he / she will want to repeat it.
- If a **learner** is **punished** for an aggressive act he / she is likely **not to repeat** it.
- Sport can be used to teach aggressive or non-aggressive acts depending on how **rewards and punishments** are used. When used effectively **sport** is seen as a very valuable way of teaching the attitudes valued by society such as:
  - **Fair play**.
  - **Cooperation**.
  - **How to cope with defeat and victory**.
  - **How to be assertive without being aggressive**.
- Unlike Instinct and Frustration-Aggression theories, **Social Learning** theory argues **against** aggression in **sport** being **cathartic** (purging of emotions). **Bandura** argues that **aggression** will only **lead to further aggression**.

Chapter 11 - INDIVIDUAL ASPECTS OF SPORT PERFORMANCE - AGGRESSION

METHODS OF ELIMINATING AGGRESSIVE TENDENCIES

- In order to eliminate aggressive tendencies we must reduce the causes of aggression.
- Earlier (page 105), the possible causes of aggression were identified as being related to an increase in arousal which could have been caused by:
  - A **physical threat** or **ego threat** (the fear of losing or the fear of looking foolish).
  - **Frustrating** circumstances.
  - The **over-emphasis on winning**.
- Aggressive behavior can also be **learned** through observational learning and modelling.
- To reduce **aggression** it must first be **prevented from occurring**. Secondly, there must be the **promotion** of **non-aggressive acts**.

PREVENT AGGRESSION

- **Reduce** the performer's **arousal** levels. Use **relaxation techniques** to avoid over-arousal, and coping strategies to deal with high levels of arousal.
- Use **punishment**, for example, taking away league points, sending players off / sin-bin.
- Employ **strong officials**.
- Make **rule changes** to outlaw further aggression, for example, sin-bin in Rugby Union. Make **rule changes** to reduce performers' **expectation of opposition aggression** thereby **reducing the tendency to retaliate first**.
- **Remove the emphasis on winning**, the coach should set performance goals rather than outcome goals (school and amateur level).
- If aggression on the field of play seems imminent, the coach should **remove transgressing players** from the pitch.
- **Reduce media sensationalisation** of aggressive acts.

PROMOTE NON-AGGRESSIVE BEHAVIOUR

- Promote **positive role models**.
- **Reward non-aggressive acts**, for example the FIFA Fair Play Award.
- Enable performers to **channel their aggression** towards a **team or individual goal** and turn reactive aggression into instrumental aggression. Suggest that the **team cause** is more **important** than individual vendettas.
- Develop a **non-aggressive ethos** within a team and emphasize peer pressure to strengthen the ethos.
- Give players **additional responsibility**, thereby decreasing the risk of the player "letting the side down".

Chapter 12 - INDIVIDUAL ASPECTS OF SPORT PERFORMANCE - ATTITUDE

Chapter 12 - INDIVIDUAL ASPECTS OF SPORT PERFORMANCE - ATTITUDE

ATTITUDE

Attitude has been defined as **a learned emotional and behavioural response to a stimulus or situation**.

- We **display attitudes** towards **attitude objects**.
- The **objects** can be **places**, **people**, and **concepts** as well as objects. Attitudes can **vary in intensity** from very weak to very strong. Attitudes are **relevant to sporting performance** because they affect the way we think, believe and **behave** in different sporting situations.

ATTITUDE FORMATION

- According to **Triandis** (1971), we **learn our attitudes** either from **direct experience** or from **other people**.
- **Direct experience** may be **pleasant** or **unpleasant** and will help us form an attitude.
- Attitudes are formed through the agents of **socialisation** (parents, teachers and friends). **Important people** in our lives can help to **shape** our attitudes. Socialisation can occur through the use of **rewards** and **punishment**, through an increase or change in a person's **knowledge** and through **peer group pressure**.
- Attitudes do **not always predict behaviour**. Just because a person possesses an opinion it does not necessarily mean he / she will behave in a certain way. **Behaviour** is often dependent on **two factors**:
    - The **expectations** of **reinforcement** and **punishment**.
    - **Social norms**, the behaviour expected in different groups of people (friends, relatives, work colleagues).

Chapter 12 - INDIVIDUAL ASPECTS OF SPORT PERFORMANCE - ATTITUDE

THE COMPONENTS OF ATTITUDE

The Cognitive Component (information)

- The **cognitive component** is the **thinking** part of an opinion.
  It is formed from any **information** a person has about an attitude object.
  It is what a person **believes** or what they **know** about an attitude object.

- For example, a basketball supporter hears that their star player is leaving to play for another team.

The Affective Component (emotion)

- The **affective component** is the **emotional response** to an attitude object, whether a person likes or dislikes it.

- For example, a basketball supporter becomes angry at hearing that the team's star player is leaving to play for another team.

The Behavioural Component

- The **behavioural component** is how a person intends to **behave towards** an attitude object.

- For example, a basketball supporter deciding to shout abuse at the player due to move to another team.

Chapter 12 - INDIVIDUAL ASPECTS OF SPORT PERFORMANCE - ATTITUDE

ATTITUDE CHANGE

- **Attitudes can be changed** by altering any of the 3 components of attitude. Attitude change is also explained by **Cognitive-Dissonance Theory** (page 115) and **Persuasive-Communication Theory** (page 116).

- The **cognitive component** can be changed by giving a person **new information**. New information will **contradict old information** and help to change attitude.
  For example, a referee who turned down an appeal for a penalty may change his opinion if he sees the foul committed on slow motion action replay.

- The **affective component** can be changed by giving a person **new experiences**. If a person dislikes an attitude object and he / she is placed in a **new situation which is enjoyable** he / she may change his / her attitude.
  For example, a person who is afraid of water is taught to swim in a warm pool with a teacher who provides gentle guidance without making him / her frightened.

- The **behavioural component** can be changed through the use of **reinforcement** and **punishment**.

- A change in **popularity** of an attitude object may also change the behaviour towards it. For example, bicycle helmets are now more popular than ever before, and bicycle clips less popular probably due to changes in the design of shorts and cycling tights.

- Attitude change is also explained by **Cognitive-Dissonance Theory** (page 115) and **Persuasive-Communication Theory** (page 116)

Chapter 12 - INDIVIDUAL ASPECTS OF SPORT PERFORMANCE - ATTITUDE

COGNITIVE-DISSONANCE THEORY - FESTINGER (1957)

- If a person holds **two ideas that are in conflict** with each other this creates discomfort. This discomfort is known as **dissonance**.
  For example:
  - The smoker who is aware of the health hazards but wants to continue smoking.
  - The team manager that wants to play new players but not drop anyone.
  - The player who wants to improve but hates training.

- A person experiencing dissonance will want to **reduce the feelings of discomfort**. This can be achieved by **lessening the impact** of one of the conflicting ideas.
  For example:
  - The smoker tries to believe that cancer will not affect him / her.
  - The team manager tries to believe that the dropped players were getting too old to play in the first team.
  - The player tries to believe that training is not really important.

- The teacher should try to **change attitudes** by **altering the 3 components of attitude** or by **changing an idea that is causing dissonance**.
  Example of Cognitive-Dissonance Theory:
  - A teacher tries to persuade a student to abseil off a bridge.
  - This particular student is the last person to try the abseil.
  - The student wants to have the satisfaction of completing the abseil but these feelings are in conflict with the feelings of not wanting to fall off the bridge and die or be seriously injured.
  - The teacher will need to get the student to concentrate on developing the feelings associated with successful completion whilst trying to reduce anxiety about falling.

Chapter 12 - INDIVIDUAL ASPECTS OF SPORT PERFORMANCE - ATTITUDE

PERSUASIVE-COMMUNICATION THEORY - KELLY (1953)

Persuasive-Communication Theory is as it sounds: one person tries to change a second person's attitude through **persuasion**. The persuader may try to give the second person **new information** or **new experiences**. Rewards or punishments may be used.

- According to Kelly **four factors affect persuasion situations**:
  - **The persuader** The persuader needs to have status, he / she needs to be perceived as being important.
  - **The message** The message needs to be presented in a way that makes others want to change their attitude.
  - **The recipients** Attitude change is easier if the recipient is easily swayed.
  - **The situation** It is easier to change an attitude if other persuaders are present, if the general mood of opinion has moved for or against an attitude object.

- Example of the **effective use of Persuasive-Communication Theory** for a teacher trying to persuade a student to abseil off a bridge:
  - **The persuader** The student trusts, respects or fears the teacher.
  - **The message** The teacher explains the situation in simple terms, and makes the prospect of abseiling at best exciting or at worst less frightening than first thought.
  - **The recipients** The student is young and impressionable.
  - **The situation** The student's friends are all supportive or have all done their abseils, and the student is the last person to go and doesn't want to look stupid by refusing.

Chapter 12 - INDIVIDUAL ASPECTS OF SPORT PERFORMANCE - ATTITUDE

THE LINK BETWEEN ATTITUDE AND BEHAVIOUR

- **Attitudes do not always predict behaviour**.

- If the cognitive and affective components of an attitude point towards a negative attitude it does not always follow that the behavioural component will be negative. **Other factors** need to be considered such as the **situation** and the **influence of other** people. The influence of the situation and others can work to increase or decrease the likelihood of a negative attitude being manifest.

The **influence of others** depends on a number of factors including:

The strength of feeling towards the attitude object:

- Increasing the **perceived importance** of the attitude object increases the likelihood of behaviour matching other components of attitude.
  For example, a student with a strong fear of water is likely to avoid swimming no matter how much pressure teachers and other students place on the student.

Degree of control:

- A person is more likely to **display behaviour** towards an attitude object if he /she feels that he /she has the **capacity to make a difference**.
  For example, a person would object to racist chanting at a football match if he / she believed that this action would stop the chanting.
  Often people say nothing because they believe their actions would make little or no difference to the behaviours of others.

- In order for a person to act he / she must believe that the **opportunity** and the **resources** are available.
  For example, a person who has a strong attitude to improve his / her fitness is more likely to start an exercise programme if he /she believes that the money and time to do so are available.

Reward and punishment:

- A person's desire to act against an attitude object often depends on the perceived likelihood of **reward** or **punishment** and on the **strength** of the reward or punishment.
  For example, some believe that rugby players are more likely to use foul play under the "sin-bin" system, whereas they would not have committed fouls when referees only had the power to send off players.

The influence of others:

- Being a **member of a group** of people or being **watched** by an **audience** can affect behaviour depending on factors such as the **size**, **proximity**, **age**, **gender**, **class** and **religion** of the audience or group. People behave differently in different groups.
  For example, swearing at a referee may be considered the norm at a football match, but not acceptable if directed at a Wimbledon umpire during a game of tennis.

Arousal level

- **Situations** can either **increase or decrease a person's arousal** level, which in turn can affect the likelihood of an attitude being displayed.
  For example, a person is less likely to hide his / her feelings when aroused.

Chapter 12 - INDIVIDUAL ASPECTS OF SPORT PERFORMANCE - ATTITUDE

PREJUDICE

- **Prejudice** is often viewed as a **negative prejudgment** about an attitude object. For an **attitude** to be **prejudicial** it is generally assumed to be **based on false information** and is unfair. In sport, **prejudice** can be seen against **officials**, **opposition**, **spectators** and **players**.

- **Prejudice** could take the form of **racial** prejudice, **sexual** prejudice or **class** prejudice.

- The prejudice may be **minor** such as not talking to an individual or excluding him / her from activities. It may go as far as the exclusion of an individual from membership of a group or club or even a particular position on a team. The prejudice may manifest itself in **more overt ways** such as chanting racist abuse at sporting events, physical threats or actual physical abuse.

METHODS TO CHALLENGE AND PREVENT PREJUDICE

- Prejudice is less likely to occur if people are given **accurate information** on which to base their opinions.

- Teachers and other **agents of socialisation** should **not be biased** or seen to be biased.

- Often, prejudice stems from a **lack of knowledge** or **understanding**. Increasing the experiences gained from people of different social and racial backgrounds will increase a person's understanding of different cultures.

- **Role models** should be used to promote **positive attitudes**.

- Individuals who are prejudicial towards others should be **punished** to prevent further prejudice.

- **Minority groups** should be given **more say**. This increases the chance of greater public understanding of minority groups.

- **Cognitive-dissonance** should be created in people with prejudice. This will increase the chance of a person rejecting a prejudicial attitude.

- The **news media** should have a responsibility to give **accurate unbiased information**.

- **Advertising campaigns** can be used to spread the non-prejudicial word.
For example, a campaign promoting girls' rugby.

Chapter 12 - INDIVIDUAL ASPECTS OF SPORT PERFORMANCE - ATTITUDE

MEASURING ATTITUDES

Generally there are three different ways to measure attitudes:

Scales and / or Questionnaires

- Attitudes can be recorded / written down using using scales such as **Thurston** scales (1931), **Likert** Scales (1932) and **Osgood** Semantic Differential Scales (1957) which identify a number of possible responses.
- Each of these scales asks for an **emotional** or **physiological response** to an attitude object.

Observing behaviour

Taking Physiological Measurements

- Such as heart rate and galvanic skin response.

TO MEASURE THE COGNITIVE COMPONENT (thoughts / knowledge)

This is concerned with how a person **categorises his / her experiences**.

Methods

- **Self-rating of knowledge** about an attitude object.
- **Statistical procedures** to identify the group of stimuli that an individual associates with an attitude object.
- **Associated thoughts** about an attitude object.
- Present the subject with a stimulus and ask him / her if the stimulus is associated with the attitude object.

TO MEASURE THE AFFECTIVE COMPONENT (emotional response)

This is concerned with measures of **likes** and **dislikes** both **physiologically** and **emotionally**.

Methods

- **Physiological responses**: heart rate, galvanic skin response, palmar sweat measures.
- **Verbal scales**, for example, Likert scales. In this type of scale, a subject is asked to ring the appropriate response to an attitude object on a questionnaire form.

Example of a Likert Scale:

- A subject may be asked to use the following scale to show his / her feelings towards an act of aggression:

A	B	C	D	E
very strong	**strong**	**mild**	**little**	**none**

Example of an Osgood Semantic Differential Scale, similar to Likert scale but easier to administer:

- A subject is asked to circle a value which closely matches his / her feeling towards fox hunting, then numerically code the answer as shown.

7	6	5	4	3	2	1
necessary	**strong**	**good**	**neutral**	**bad**	**weak**	**unnecessary**

Chapter 12 - INDIVIDUAL ASPECTS OF SPORT PERFORMANCE - ATTITUDE

TO MEASURE THE BEHAVIOURAL COMPONENT

Methods:

- **Direct observation** of behaviour.
- Use of a **verbal scale**.

The problem is that **behaviour** is only **partly determined by attitude**. To measure the attitude component, other components (norms, habits, expectations of reinforcements) have to be **controlled**. This is difficult.

Example of a Behavioural Differential Scale measuring behavioural intention towards people

- A student is asked how he / she would behave towards a PE teacher who asked him / her to perform a front somersault.

I would	**a) follow the request without question**	**I would not**
I would	**b) ask the teacher to give further information**	**I would not**
I would	**c) refuse the request**	**I would not**

A student questionnaire enquiring as to attitude to physical activity is located on page 174.

Chapter 13 - INDIVIDUAL ASPECTS OF SPORT PERFORMANCE - MOTIVATION

Chapter 13 - INDIVIDUAL ASPECTS OF SPORT PERFORMANCE - MOTIVATION

MOTIVATION

Stallings (1966) has defined **motivation** as **an internal factor** that **arouses** and **directs behaviour**.

- **Motivation** is the **power** or **drive** behind why we do something.
- **Motivation** is responsible for:
  - The **selection** and **preference** for an activity.
  - The **persistence** at the activity.
  - The **intensity** and **effort** put into performance.

TYPES OF MOTIVATION

- **Intrinsic Motivation** — Feelings from **inside ourselves**. For example, fun, enjoyment, joy, satisfaction.
- **Extrinsic Motivation** — Feelings coming from gaining **external rewards** both **physical** (money, trophies) and **emotional** (praise).
- **Primary Motivation** — Primary motivation is derived **from the activity itself**.
- **Secondary Motivation** — Secondary motivation comes from **anything other than taking part**. For example, from coach or friends, from winning medals.
- **Positive and Negative Motivation** — **Any aspect of competing** can have a positive or negative effect on motivation. Winning is positively motivating, losing can be negatively motivating. An audience can have either a positive or a negative effect.

Chapter 13 - INDIVIDUAL ASPECTS OF SPORT PERFORMANCE - MOTIVATION

MEASURING MOTIVATION

1. Tutko and Richards (1972) **Motivational Rating Scale**

❒ These workers measured **11 traits** which contributed to the motivation of **highly successful athletes**:

- ❒ **Aggression**
- ❒ **Coachability**
- ❒ **Emotional Control**
- ❒ **Mental Toughness**
- ❒ **Drive**
- ❒ **Self-confidence**
- ❒ **Determination**
- ❒ **Leadership**
- ❒ **Responsibility**
- ❒ **Trust**
- ❒ **Conscientiousness**

2. Kenyon (1968) **Attitude Towards Physical Activity Inventory**

❒ Kenyon measured **6 reasons** why people **take part in physical activity**:

- ❒ **Social**
- ❒ **Heath and Fitness**
- ❒ **Vertigo (excitement)**
- ❒ **Aesthetic**
- ❒ **Ascetic (physical challenge)**
- ❒ **Catharsis (relaxation)**

3. Alderman and Wood (1976) **Incentive Motivation Inventory**

❒ These workers measured **7 reasons** why people **take part in physical activity**:

- ❒ **Affiliation**
- ❒ **Aggression**
- ❒ **Excellence**
- ❒ **Independence**
- ❒ **Power**
- ❒ **Stress**
- ❒ **Success**

Chapter 13 - INDIVIDUAL ASPECTS OF SPORT PERFORMANCE - MOTIVATION

ACHIEVEMENT MOTIVATION

Achievement motivation is defined as a fundamental **drive to succeed** or persist with a task. According to Atkinson (1974), whenever a person is faced with a task, the **decision to accept or reject** the task is based on both **personality** and **situational** factors.

THE PERSONALITY FACTORS

- **The need to achieve** (**Nach**) is the factor which causes a person to **strive** in order to gain **pride** or **satisfaction**.
- **The need to avoid failure** (**Naf**) is the factor which causes a person to **try hard** in order to **avoid shame** and **humiliation**.
- In any **challenging situation** everyone will have **both Nach** and **Naf**. Whichever feeling is **strongest** will determine whether the task is accepted or rejected.
- **High achievers** have **high Nach** and **low Naf**; they concentrate on **success** and **do not worry about failure**.
- **Low achievers** have **low Nach** and **high Naf**; they worry about how they will feel if they fail.

THE SITUATIONAL FACTORS

- **The incentive value of success** (**Is**) and the **incentive value of failure** (**If**).
- **The probability of success** (**Ps**) and the **probability of failure** (**Pf**).
- The **incentive value** of a task to a person is how much the individual thinks he / she will **gain** or **lose** by accepting the task. **Is** is **inversely proportional** to **Ps**, in other words as **Ps** increases **Is** reduces.
  For example, the **Ps** for a hole in one at golf is very small so the **Is** is huge.

THE COMBINATION OF PERSONALITY AND SITUATIONAL FACTORS

- The **personality** factors when **combined** with the **situational** factors result in a person having :
  - **The tendency to approach success** (**Ts**).
  - **The tendency to avoid failure** (**Taf**).

$$Ts = Nach \times Ps \times Is$$
$$Taf = Naf \times Pf \times If$$

- Whichever of the two tendencies is **strongest** will determine whether a task is accepted or rejected.

Chapter 13 - INDIVIDUAL ASPECTS OF SPORT PERFORMANCE - MOTIVATION

IMPLICATIONS FOR THE COACH

A coach wants an **athlete** to have a **high tendency to approach success** and a **low tendency to avoid failure**.

- What can the coach do to **improve Ts** and **reduce Taf**?
  - **Manipulate the personality factors by improving Nach and reducing Naf**.
  - **Manipulate the situational factors**.
- **Increase Nach** by **increasing** the amount of **positive reinforcement** thus increasing the feelings of pride and satisfaction associated with success.
- **Reduce Naf** by **reducing punishment** and stop the performer worrying about failure, thus reducing the negative feelings associated with failure.
- **Reduce Naf** by **focusing negative feedback** on **effort** rather than ability. The performer will then know that he / she can do better next time. This will reduce the chance of "learned helplessness".
- Any **task** set should have a **choice of difficulty** so that everyone can achieve success at the level of their choice. If a single difficult task is set, those with high Naf may not want to try.
- Get the **low achiever used to succeeding** by placing him / her in situations where success is guaranteed, then **gradually increase the task difficulty**. Any **failures** should be **attributed** to **lack of effort** rather than ability.
- Try **not to place** the performer in situations where **defeat** is inevitable. If this is unavoidable, **alter the criteria for success**.
  For example, in a Badminton match, success would be “not lose by more than five points in each game”.
- To sustain motivation in those performers with high Nach, **tasks** set should be **challenging**.
- Achieve the **correct level of Ps** to ensure adequate motivation.
  - **Too easy** and the task will be **boring**.
  - **Too hard** and the task will be **impossible**.
- Achieve the **correct level of Is**, too little and the task will be pointless.

QUESTIONNAIRE

- An **student achievement motivation questionnaire** which assesses this broad factor, is found on page 175 Appendix 2 of this guide.

Chapter 13 - INDIVIDUAL ASPECTS OF SPORT PERFORMANCE - MOTIVATION

ACHIEVEMENT MOTIVATION AND SPORT

Much of achievement motivation theory was developed outside sport. To get a **sporting perspective** on the theory we must find out if a person's desire to accept a challenge differs if the challenge is a sporting challenge.

- Sport is different from everyday life. We cannot guarantee that a person who is **very competitive** when he / she plays sport will be **equally competitive** in **other areas of life**.
- In order to accurately measure achievement motivation, we need to find out what it is that makes sporting challenges **different** from everyday life.
- Alderman and Wood (1976) identified **seven main reasons** why a person would accept a **sporting challenge**:
  - **The need for affiliation (social)**.
  - **The need to exert aggression**.
  - **The need to be independent**.
  - **The need to exert power**.
  - **The need to seek out stress**.
  - **The need to succeed**.
- Work by **Gill** (1988) has shown that whilst all people have a need to succeed, they may have **different measures** of success. We set ourselves **different goals** to **measure success** and **failure**. To understand achievement motivation in sport we must find out **what performers use to measure success**.

COMPETITIVE ORIENTATION

- According to Gill (2000), sporting behaviour is competitive behaviour, and in order to assess achievement motivation in sport we must **examine competitive behaviour**. Gill developed a **questionnaire** to measure **competitive orientation**, the **Sport Orientation Questionnaire (SOQ)**.
- **SOQ** measured three components of competitiveness:
  - The feelings derived from the **competition itself**.
  - The feelings associated with **winning and losing**.
  - The feelings associated with **task mastery**.
- The results suggested that **sport performers** were **more competitive** than non-performers. More surprising was the result that **sport performers** were more likely to be driven by **performance goals** and less likely to be motivated by winning outcomes. **Coaches** should therefore attempt to **set tasks** which require increasing levels of **competency**, not simply tasks that require the performer to win.

GOAL-PERSPECTIVE THEORY

- An alternative to Gill's work is found in **Goal-Perspective Theory**. According to the theory, performers are motivated in two ways:
  - **Task-oriented performers** are driven by the need to **master a task**.
  - **Ego-oriented performers** are driven by the **need to succeed** against other people.
- **Sport** gives the opportunity for both **task** and **ego-oriented** performers. **Coaches** should set **tasks** which appeal to those performers who want to **master certain skills**, and also set tasks which allow for performers to **compete** against each other.

Chapter 13 - INDIVIDUAL ASPECTS OF SPORT PERFORMANCE - MOTIVATION

ATTRIBUTION THEORY (WEINER 1974)

Attribution theory is concerned with the **reasons** (**attributions**) performers give to their **success or failure**.

- Weiner suggested that **high achievers** and **low achievers** attribute **success** and **failure** to **different reasons**. Consequently, **to become a high achiever** the performer must **think like a high achiever**, the performer must make attributions like a high achiever.

- **Weiner's 4 Attributions**:
    - **Ability**.
    - **Effort**.
    - **Luck**.
    - **Task Difficulty**.

- The 4 attributions can be placed along **2 dimensions**:
    - **Locus of causality**.
    - **Stability**.

THE MODEL

		Locus of Causality	
		INTERNAL	EXTERNAL
Stability	STABLE	Ability	Task Difficulty
	UNSTABLE	Effort	Luck

- The **Locus of Causality** dimension refers to whether the performance outcome could be caused by **factors under the control** of the performer (**the internal factors of effort and ability**), or caused by **factors beyond the control** of the performer (**the external factors of task difficulty and luck**).

- The **Stability** dimension refers to whether the performance outcome is **fixed and unchanging** or can **vary over time**. **Ability** and **task difficulty** are **stable and fixed** during the period of performance. **Effort** and **luck** may **change from performance to performance** or within the performance.

Chapter 13 - INDIVIDUAL ASPECTS OF SPORT PERFORMANCE - MOTIVATION

ATTRIBUTION THEORY - THE MAIN POINTS

- Individuals often make **internal attributions for success** and **external attributions for failure**. We like to feel that **we are responsible for success** but that **failure** was due to **factors beyond our control**.

- The **stability** dimension in this theory is usually seen to be related to **future expectations**. If we **attribute success or failure** to **stable factors**, then next time we compete we will expect the **same result**.

- High and Low achievers attribute success and failure to **different factors**.

- **High achievers** tend to attribute **success** to **internal factors** and **failure** to **unstable factors**.

- **Low achievers** tend to attribute **success** to **external factors** and **failure** to **stable factors**.

- **Girls** tend to have attributions consistent with those of **low achievers**. **Boys** tend to have higher expectations of **success**.

QUESTIONNAIRE

- An **student attribution questionnaire** which assesses this broad factor, is found on page 176 / 177 Appendix 3 of this guide.

Chapter 13 - INDIVIDUAL ASPECTS OF SPORT PERFORMANCE - MOTIVATION

ATTRIBUTION THEORY AND ACHIEVEMENT MOTIVATION - WHAT CAN IT BE USED FOR?

- The **coach** should try to make the performer:
    - Attribute **success** to **internal factors** in order to maximise confidence and satisfaction.
    - Attribute **success** to **stable factors** in order to maximise the expectation of future success.
    - Attribute **failure** to **external factors** in order to minimise negative feelings.
    - Attribute **failure** to **unstable factors** in order to minimise the expectations of future losses. Be careful when attributing failure to lack of effort if the performer has tried their hardest.
    - **Redefine success** where **ability** is the **reason for failure**.
    - Acknowledge the need to **change attributions** (called **attribution retraining**) to those appropriate to high achievers.
    - If a **low achiever**, learn how to attribute success and failure to the **same reasons** given by **high achievers**.
    - Be aware that low achievers often suffer from **Learned Helplessness**.

LEARNED HELPLESSNESS

- **Learned helplessness** is the **acquired belief** that a person has **no control** over **negative events**, that **failure is inevitable**. Performers with learned helplessness will need **attribution retraining**. Their **confidence levels** will need to be **increased** along with a belief that they can control their own destiny.
- **Low achievers** will need **attribution retraining**.

SELF-EFFICACY

- **Self-efficacy** is a **situational form of self-confidence**. **High achievers** often have **high** levels of **self-efficacy**.
- Studies have suggested that when all else is equal the performer with the highest self-efficacy will win. **Coaches** should try to **encourage self-efficacy**.

Chapter 13 - INDIVIDUAL ASPECTS OF SPORT PERFORMANCE - MOTIVATION

Chapter 14 - GROUP DYNAMICS OF SPORT PERFORMANCE - GROUPS AND TEAMS

Chapter 14 - GROUP DYNAMICS OF SPORT PERFORMANCE - GROUPS AND TEAMS

GROUPS

According to Carron (1980), a **group** has the following characteristics:

- **A collective identity**.
- **A sense of shared purpose**.
- **Structured patterns of communication**.

- A **successful team** is one which maximises the characteristics listed above.
- A **successful team** has good **cohesion**. **Cohesion** is the **motivation** that keeps group members together and which inhibits the break up of the group. Group members may be **motivated to be in the group** because of the **success** it brings them or because they **value the relationships** within the group.
- A coach must use a knowledge of groups and group dynamics to make the team function more effectively.

STEINER'S MODEL OF GROUP PERFORMANCE

- According to **Steiner** (1972):

  Actual group performance = potential productivity - losses due to faulty processes

- Terms are defined as follows:

Potential productivity	The group's best performance given its resources (skill, knowledge).
Faulty processes	Things that can go wrong.

- **Two main reasons** exist for **faulty processes**:

Coordination losses	Due to the team not working effectively together. For example, through poor timing or strategy.
Motivation losses	Due to team members losing the will to do their best.

- The coach will need to put together a group with **high potential productivity** whilst trying to **minimise losses** due to faulty processes.
- **Minimising losses could be achieved by**:
  - Organising practices so that all **team members are certain of their role**.
  - **Overlearning set plays** in order to get the timing right.
  - Manipulating the **use of rewards** to optimise **motivation** levels.
- Coaches should **not just pick the best players** for a team, but those who are most likely to **get on with each other**.

Chapter 14 - GROUP DYNAMICS OF SPORT PERFORMANCE - GROUPS AND TEAMS

THE RINGLEMANN EFFECT AND SOCIAL LOAFING

According to **Ringlemann**, individual **performance decreases** with an **increase in group size**. From studies into tug-of-war it was found that an eight did not pull eight times as hard as solo pullers.

- According to **Latane** (1979), **social loafing** is said to occur when an individual suffers **motivational losses** within a group. The individual feels that a reduction in effort would not be noticed. He / she can **hide within the group** and take it easy.

AVOIDING SOCIAL LOAFING

A coach will need to **discourage social loafing**. This can be done by trying to make sure that team members' **contributions are valued**.

- **Highlight individual performance**.
  For example, the use of statistics in basketball (shooting, rebounding and assists).
- **Positively reinforce** good team and individual performances.
- Foster **team spirit**, if each team member feels they are part of the team, social loafing can be reduced.
- Assign **individual roles** and **responsibilities**.
- Heighten the importance of **units** within teams.
  For example, the defensive unit in hockey.
- Make **players** who are loafing **aware** of it.
  For example, talk to them or even substitute them in a game.
- Increase the **social support** given by other team members.

OTHER WAYS OF IMPROVING GROUP SUCCESS

- Ensure **team members** know their **responsibilities**.
- Provide opportunities to **socialise**.
- Ensure **team members' contributions** are **valued** and **rewarded**.
- Share **ownership** of ideas. **Discussion** is more likely to bring **consensus**. Team members will work harder if ideas are **not** imposed.
- Emphasise **group goals**.

Chapter 14 - GROUP DYNAMICS OF SPORT PERFORMANCE - GROUPS AND TEAMS

COHESION

Festinger (1950) stated that **cohesion** is the **total field of forces** which act upon members to **remain** in the group.

- **Cohesion** or cohesiveness is the **glue that sticks members of a group together**. It consists of the reasons why members work with each other through the good and the bad.

FACTORS AFFECTING THE FORMATION AND DEVELOPMENT OF A COHESIVE TEAM

Research suggests that **cohesiveness** is related to **team success** for interactive team sports. **Successful teams** are often very **cohesive**, but we must take care as it does not necessarily follow that a cohesive team will be successful.

- In order to devise ways of **developing team cohesion**, we must first understand how cohesion is formed. According to Weinberg (1992), early cohesion research focused on two dimensions, **task cohesion** and **social cohesion**.
  - **Task Cohesion** — The way in which team members **work with each other** to successfully **complete** a task.
  - **Social Cohesion** — The way in which team members **work with each other** to develop and **maintain relationships** within the group.

- **Teachers and coaches** will need to develop task and social cohesion.
  - **Task Cohesion** — Identify a **team goal** and find ways to get team members to **remember** the team goal, **value** it and **strive to achieve** it.

    For example, the work ethic or "pass and move" system of play promoted by Premiership Football teams.
  - **Social Cohesion** — Create opportunities for **social development**, promote an **interesting** and **enjoyable** environment where players can **interact positively** with each other, make friends and have fun.

    For example, the "crazy gang" at Wimbledon F.C. or the team spirit of The British Lions Rugby team.

Chapter 14 - GROUP DYNAMICS OF SPORT PERFORMANCE - GROUPS AND TEAMS

CARRON (1982) CONCEPTUAL MODEL FOR COHESION

Carron has been one of the major writers on the development of cohesion. The model below outlines **four factors** affecting the development of **cohesion**:

- **Environmental factors**.
- **Personal factors**.
- **Team factors**.
- **Leadership factors**.

Environmental Factors	Factors which **bind a player** to a team. For example, contracts, location, age and eligibility restrictions.
Personal Factors	Factors which an individual believes are important and **keep him / her in the team.** These could be the need to **win** or be **successful**, the need for **affiliation** (social reasons), or the need for **excellence**.
Leadership Factors	The **behaviours** of **coaches** and leaders which aid in team cohesion. **Coaches** can **promote** both task and social cohesion.
Team Factors	Factors related **solely to the group** such as **team identity**, the **targets** the team sets itself, the **ability** of the team members and the **role** of each team member.

Chapter 14 - GROUP DYNAMICS OF SPORT PERFORMANCE - GROUPS AND TEAMS

CARRON (1982) CONCEPTUAL MODEL FOR COHESION (continued)

With a knowledge of Carron's four factors affecting team cohesiveness we can find ways to **develop cohesiveness** in a team.

- **Environmental Factors**

  Try to **treat all players equally** and avoid a "star" system.

  Where possible make players' **contracts uniform** (similar from one player to another).

  Use **tours** to allow players living in different locations to **train** and **socialise** together for extended periods.

- **Personal Factors**

  A coach needs to **discover** each team member's **reasons** for wanting to be in the group (task or social cohesion), and try to **give opportunities** for the **expression** or **realisation** of the motive.

  Develop a feeling of **ownership** amongst the players.

  Players will be more likely to show **increased effort** and **responsibility** if they believe the team is "**their**" **team**.

  Particular **social groupings** should be encouraged, for example, young players learning from older players.

  Some **groupings** should be **avoided**, **player exclusion may increase** if certain "**cliques**" are allowed to develop.

- **Leadership Factors**

  According to Chelladurai a coach can display **five leadership behaviours**:

  Training and instruction.
  Democratic.
  Autocratic.
  Social support.
  Rewarding.

  A coach will need to display all these five types of behaviour.

  Players are **all different** and a team may have individuals who separately value a different type of behaviour from a coach.

- **Team Factors**

  A team should have **short**, **medium** and **long-term goals** to provide direction and motivation.

  Individual roles should be prescribed and **methods** to **measure** and **reward** individual efforts should be devised.

  A **rewards** and **punishment** system could be implemented to develop team identity and to set behaviours.

Chapter 14 - GROUP DYNAMICS OF SPORT PERFORMANCE - GROUPS AND TEAMS

GROUPS

A group involves **two or more people** who are **interacting with one another** in such a manner that each person influences and is influenced by the other(s) (Shaw - 1976).

- The term **Group Dynamics** describes the processes within a group and between group members (Honeybourne).
- By studying **group dynamics** a coach can try to identify **factors** which affect **cohesion** and then take measures to improve cohesion.
- **Cohesion** has been defined as the extent to which members of the group exhibit a **desire** to achieve **common goals** and **group identity**.
- In order to identify cohesion a coach will need to assess **interaction**. Carron has represented interaction in diagrammatic form.

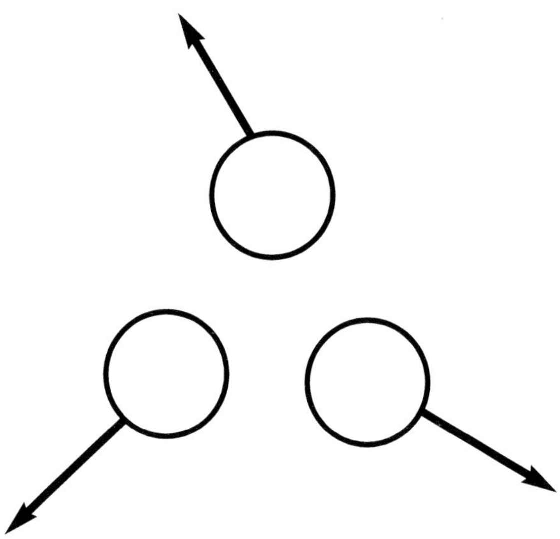

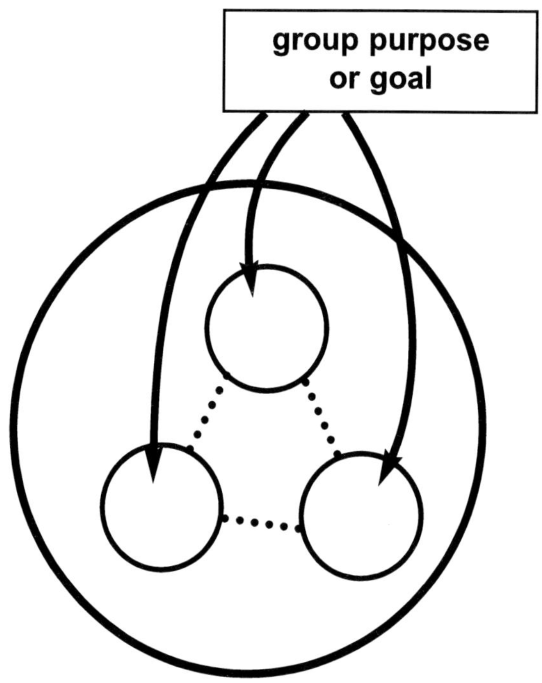

Separate individuals have no interaction and have independent behaviour.

Any view looks outward from the group and the interests of other group members are ignored.

..... = Group processes such as interaction, personal and task interdependence, and communication.

The large circle represents a collective identity, with a sense of shared purpose.

Chapter 14 - GROUP DYNAMICS OF SPORT PERFORMANCE - GROUPS AND TEAMS

SOCIOGRAMS

Sociograms are used to show **patterns of friendship**. Each team member is asked to name up to two others they would choose as friends.

- The diagram below shows the **choices of an imaginary team**.

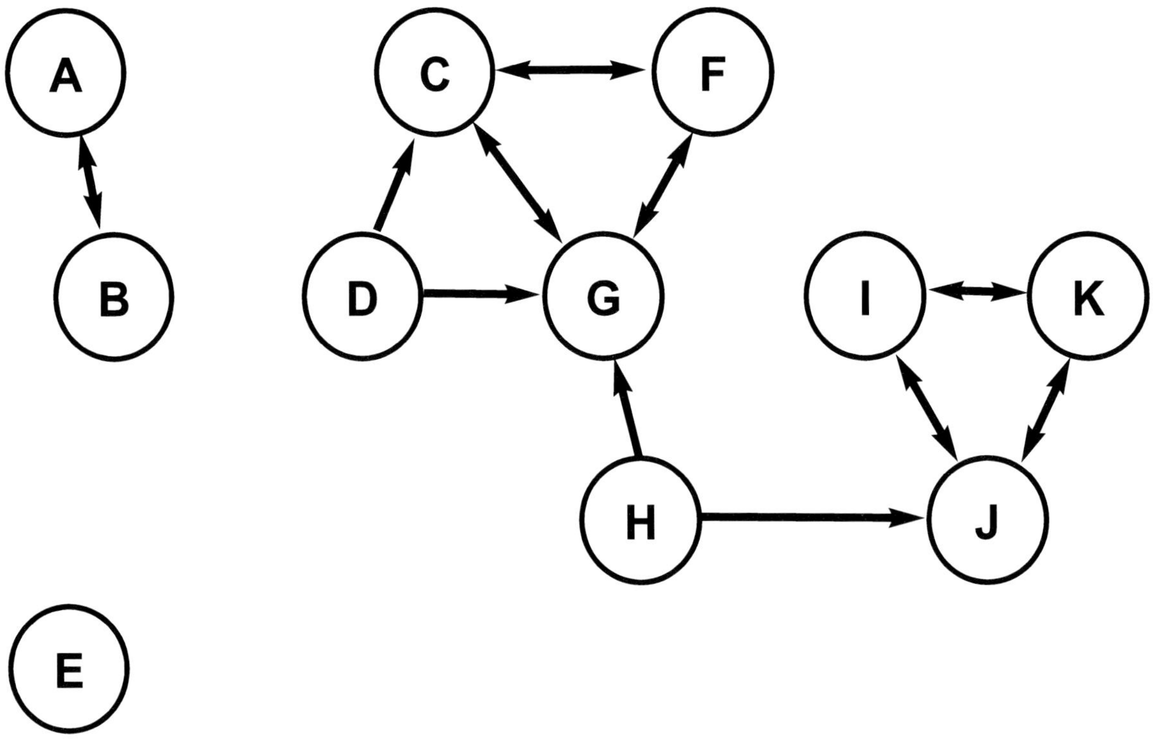

The diagram can be used to **identify certain characters** within the team:

- **Star** Someone who is chosen by many (G).
- **Pair or Diad** Two people who choose each other (A, B).
- **Three or Triad** Three people who choose each other (I, J, K).
- **Isolate** Someone who does not make a choice (E).
- **Rejectee** Someone who is not chosen by anyone (D, H, E).

- Once the **characters** have been **identified**, the **coach** may want to adopt **strategies** to **strengthen** or **lessen** the **links** between certain team members in order to improve cohesion.

- Finally we must ask the question: are successful **teams successful** because they are **cohesive** or are they cohesive because they are successful?

Chapter 15 - GROUP DYNAMICS OF SPORT PERFORMANCE - LEADERSHIP

Chapter 15 - GROUP DYNAMICS OF SPORT PERFORMANCE - LEADERSHIP

LEADERSHIP

Leadership is defined by Barrow (1977) as "**The process of influencing individuals and groups towards set goals**".

- An **effective leader** can set **challenging goals** and **devise methods** to achieve the goals. An **effective leader** can **use a range of methods** to get team members to perform to the best of their ability.
  - According to **Trait Theory** leaders are **born** with the **skill** needed to lead.
  - According to **Social Learning theory** leaders **learn** the **skills** needed to lead.
  - According to **Interactionist Theory**, leadership qualities can come as a result of **inherited abilities and learned** skills.
- Leaders can become leaders in a number of ways. Carron (1981) identified **two ways** in which a person could become a leader:
  - **Emergent leaders** come from within the group. They emerge due to their skill level and the wishes of group members.
    For example, a team captain or pack leader elected by the team.
  - **Prescribed leaders** are appointed.
    For example, a teacher, coach or manager.

LEADERSHIP TYPES

authoritarian	democratic	laissez-faire

Strict--Relaxed

- The **authoritarian leader** makes **all the decisions** and is often motivated by the **successful completion of a task**. **Decisions** will be made **quickly** but often members will feel upset that they are not part of the decision making process. This type of leader is often **afraid of giving over power** to team members.
- The **democratic leader shares the decision making** and is often interested in **developing meaningful relationships** within the team. **Team members** often **work harder** if they have "**ownership**" of a task. This type of leadership can often result in decisions being made **slowly**.
- The **laissez-faire leader** sits back and **lets others make decisions**. This type of leader is often interested in developing the **problem-solving** capabilities of team members. This leadership style could be used when the **leader lacks confidence** or is lazy. The main problem with this leadership style is that **teams can lack direction** or **drive** or a **leadership** figure.
- **Each leadership type** can be **effective** in **different situations**.

Chapter 15 - GROUP DYNAMICS OF SPORT PERFORMANCE - LEADERSHIP

LEADERSHIP MODELS

CHELLADURAI'S MULTIDIMENSIONAL MODEL (1984)

According to Chelladurai there are **five types of leadership behaviour**:

❒ **Training and Instruction**	Behaviour aimed at improving performance.
❒ **Democratic**	Allows decisions to be made collectively.
❒ **Autocratic**	Personal authority.
❒ **Social support**	Concern for the well-being of others.
❒ **Rewarding**	Positive reinforcement.

- These behaviours can be measured using the **Leadership Scale for Sport** (**LSS**). See an example of an **LSS** on page 178, Appendix 4 below.
- A **good leader** will need to demonstrate **all five types** of behaviour.
- The leader's **behaviour** is **only one factor** that controls a person's ability to lead.

Chelladurai states that there are **three factors** that control a persons **ability** to lead:

❒ **Situation characteristics**	**Environmental conditions** such as whether the leader leads individuals or groups, the time the group has spent together, the type of task.
❒ **Leader characteristics**	The **type of leader** (autocratic, democratic).
❒ **Member characteristics**	The **players preferred** leadership style and their expectations.

- The leader will be **most effective** when these three factors are compatible. For example, when the **situation** calls for a leader to take charge, when the **leader's style** is autocratic, and when the **members** prefer their leader to be autocratic.

Chapter 15 - GROUP DYNAMICS OF SPORT PERFORMANCE - LEADERSHIP

FIEDLER'S CONTINGENCY MODEL (1967)

According to **Fiedler**, the **effectiveness** of a leader is dependent on 2 factors:

- **The personality of the coach**.
- **The situation**.

- The personality of the leader is **measured** using **The Least Preferred Co-worker Scale** (**LPC**). The test records whether a leader is **task-orientated** (concerned with achievement) or **person-orientated** (concerned with the members of the group). See an example of a **student LPC** on page 179 Appendix 5 below.
- The **type of situation** is said to determine which type of leader will be most successful.
- According to Fiedler:
    - A **task-orientated** leader is most successful in the most favourable and least favourable situations.
    - A **person-orientated** leader is most successful in moderately favourable situations.

Situation	Characteristics	Example
Most Favourable	Relationships are warm, the task has a clear structure, and the leader is powerful.	The manager of a very successful football team would have developed a clear structure to training, diet, individual and unit roles and team strategy. The team is winning so the players are happy. The manager has the respect of the players and the power to hire, fire, reward and punish.
Moderately Favourable	Relationships are warm, players are enthusiastic but not gifted, resources are limited, the task has little structure.	The manager of a local club team with poor resources, little ambition, and players who just want to have fun. A person-orientated leader will be effective in creating an enjoyable atmosphere and get the best from players who are not willing to conform to a strict training regime.
Least Favourable	Relationships have broken down, the task has no clearly defined structure and the leader has little or no power.	The manager of a football team facing relegation has lost the respect of the players. The players are frustrated at losing. The coaching methods are not working and a new direction is needed. Usually the result would be for the Chairman to appoint a new manager, an authoritarian leader with new ideas and the power to force people to follow him.

Chapter 16 - GROUP DYNAMICS OF SPORT PERFORMANCE - SOCIAL FACILITATION

Chapter 16 - GROUP DYNAMICS OF SPORT PERFORMANCE - SOCIAL FACILITATION

SOCIAL FACILITATION AND AUDIENCE EFFECTS

Social Facilitation has been defined as: **"The consequences upon behaviour which derive from the mere presence of others."** Zajonc (1965)

❒ The term **others** may mean **other performers** or an **audience**.

❒ The **audience** may be **silent** or **noisy**.

❒ The **effect** that other people can have on **performance** could be:
  - ❒ **Positive**.
  - ❒ **Negative**.
  - ❒ **Neutral**.

❒ Often the term **social inhibition** is used to mean the **negative affect** of others **on performance**.

❒ Whilst **social facilitation** has more recently been used to mean the **positive effects** of others **on performance**.

❒ The name given to **fellow performers** is **coactors**.

DRIVE THEORY TO EXPLAIN THE EFFECT OF AUDIENCE

❒ The **effect** of others on performance is to **increase arousal**. This increase in arousal can have a **positive** or **negative effect on performance**.

❒ Zajonc's work used **drive theory** to explain the effect of others on performance. He proposed that the **effect of others** was to **increase arousal** or **drive**.

❒ An **increase in arousal** was said to bring about the **dominant** (most likely) **response**.

❒ For a **well-learned task** the **dominant response** is likely to be **correct**.
If the task is **not well-learned** the **dominant response** is likely to be **incorrect**.

Level of Learning	Effect of others on performance	Example
❒ **Well-learned**	Increase in arousal bringing about a (correct) dominant response.	Top athletes produce their best performances under the pressure of competition and with a big crowd.
❒ **Not well-learned**	Increase in arousal bringing about a (incorrect) dominant response.	Students' often say to their teacher "Don't watch me, I always make a mistake when you watch me."

SOCIAL FACILITATION AND AUDIENCE EFFECTS (continued)

FACTORS AFFECTING THE EFFECT OF AUDIENCE

The effect the audience has on performance depends on a number of factors:

Factor	Effect
❐ **Size of audience**	**Larger crowds** will **increase arousal**.
❐ **Proximity to the performers**	The **closer** the audience the **larger** the increase in **arousal**.
❐ **Intentions of the audience**	This can cause a **positive** or **negative** effect depending on the personality of the performer.
❐ **Level of learning of the task**	**Performance** will generally **increase** if the task is well-learned, and will decrease if the task is not fully-learned.
❐ **Personality of the performer**	**Extroverts** perform **better** when **aroused**, introverts can easily be over-aroused.
❐ **Type of task**	**Gross motor skills benefit** from **increased arousal** levels, **fine motor skills** need **low levels** of arousal.

Chapter 16 - GROUP DYNAMICS OF SPORT PERFORMANCE - SOCIAL FACILITATION

EVALUATION APPREHENSION

Cottrell (1965) used the term **evaluation apprehension** to describe the effect on performance caused by the performer's **perceived intentions of the audience**.

- If the performer perceives that others are evaluating his / her performance, an increased level of arousal will result. The **performer is apprehensive** because he / she **believes** that the **audience will evaluate his / her performance**.

- This can have a negative effect on performance. Conversely, if the performer believes the **audience to be supportive**, this could lead to an **improvement in performance**.

HOMEFIELD ADVANTAGE

Large **supportive home crowds** are supposed to give the **home team** an **advantage**. This is known as the **homefield advantage**.

- Research has suggested that results in most sports are better for teams playing at home, especially for **indoor sports** such as Ice Hockey and Basketball. **Large supportive crowds** may contribute to **improved performance**, but it cannot be said they are the main cause of the homefield advantage. Other factors, such as the effects of travel and unfamiliar surroundings, have to be considered.

SOCIAL INHIBITION

Social inhibition is the term used to describe the **negative** effect of others on **performance**.

- The effect of an audience on performance is to increase arousal. The **coach** will need to **manage** the performer's **arousal level** in order to **minimise** the effects of **social inhibition**. This can be achieved in a number of ways.

METHODS TO COMBAT SOCIAL INHIBITION

- Ensure that skills are developed **away from an audience**, in a **low pressure** environment.
- Develop a performer's powers of **selective attention** in order for him / her to concentrate on important information and **avoid** being **distracted** by the audience.
- Use **anxiety management techniques** (relaxation, thought stopping) to **reduce** arousal levels.
- Use **mental rehearsal** by performers in order to **practise** any socially inhibiting situation and **rehearse** previously learned coping strategies.
  For example, if a player is receiving abuse from the crowd, he can rerun the situation in his mind and practise selective attention techniques to keep focused on his role.
- Use **practice sessions** to develop **audience coping strategies**.
  For example, the England Rugby team used to listen to opposition national anthems on the bus on the way to the match to prepare for crowd noise.
- Take **young players** to large events to "**acclimatise**".
  For example, young British tennis players often accompany the Davis Cup team.

Chapter 17 - MENTAL PREPARATION for SPORT PERFORMANCE - COMMITMENT

Chapter 17 - MENTAL PREPARATION for SPORT PERFORMANCE - COMMITMENT

MENTAL PREPARATION FOR SPORT PERFORMANCE

The organisation "**sportscoachUK**" (**SCUK**) formerly known as the **National Coaching Foundation** (**NCF**) is a support service for sports organisations and coaches providing coaching courses, advice and information and specialist expertise from the likes of top sports scientists.

- In the NCF publication "Psychology and Performance", the NCF aims to highlight and seeks to develop a number of mental qualities needed by the sports performer.
- These **mental qualities** are termed the **four C's**:
    - **Commitment** to work towards goals.
    - **Confidence** (self) in a performer's ability to succeed.
    - **Control** (emotional) to focus energy on the goal.
    - **Concentration**.

Chapter 17 - MENTAL PREPARATION for SPORT PERFORMANCE - COMMITMENT

COMMITMENT

All sports players have **dreams** and **aspirations**. The role of the **coach** is to **channel a player's commitment** towards his / her dreams.

- The coach will first attempt to identify **measurable goals** in the **short**, **medium** and **long-term**. In this way the performer will have something **tangible to aim** for.

GOALS AND GOAL SETTING

- The **long-term goal** could be the performer's **original dream**. By breaking the long-term goal into **short-term goals** (daily or weekly) and **medium-term goals** (monthly or annually), the performer is able to achieve success on a regular basis. This in turn will **help build confidence** and **commitment**.

- The importance of **goal setting** has been highlighted by the **SCUK**, who has reported that the **successful attainment of goals** will help to increase **motivation** and **self-confidence**, focus **attention** and reduce **anxiety**.

- Gill's (2000) summary of research findings related to **goal setting** found that:
    - Sports performers who were good at **setting performance** (**improvement**) **goals** were **less anxious** and **performed better** than those performers who set **outcome goals**.
    - **Specific**, **difficult**, and **challenging goals** improve performance more than do-your-best general goals.

TYPES OF GOALS

It can be seen from the results above that there are a number of **different types** of goal. Broadly speaking, goals can be divided into two types: **outcome** and **performance** goals.

Outcome Goals

- **Outcome Goals** relate to the final outcome of performance, **winning** or **losing**. Outcome goals are often **externally** controlled. Winning or losing are often determined by factors such as the **quality of opposition** or **luck**.

Performance Goals

- **Performance Goals** relate to **measurable results** of performance: how far, how fast, how high, how many. **Process** (performance) **Goals** are generally **under the control of the performer** and relate to the performer's effort or ability.

- It is **easier** to set **performance** goals because they are **easier to achieve** and are a truer reflection of the performer's commitment to training and competition. Because of this they can often be **more motivational** than outcome goals.
  For example, it is often more pleasing to set and attain the target of a personal best in the Olympics, than to set a target of winning and not even make the final.

Chapter 17 - MENTAL PREPARATION for SPORT PERFORMANCE - COMMITMENT

SMARTER GOALS

The SCUK (NCF) have used the acronym **SMARTER** to describe the qualities needed for the effective setting of process goals.

(Adapted from NCF (1996) "Psychology and Performance").

- ❒ **Specific** Should be as specific as possible to focus attention.
- ❒ **Measurable** To assess progress against a standard.
- ❒ **Accepted** By both the performer and coach.
- ❒ **Realistic** Challenging but within the performer's capability.
- ❒ **Time phased** With a specific date for completion.
- ❒ **Exciting** Inspiring, challenging and rewarding to the performer.
- ❒ **Recorded** Written down by the performer and coach to evaluate progress, and to provide feedback and motivation.

Examples from Specific Sports of SMARTER Applications

	Hockey	Badminton	Athletics
❒ **Specific**	To beat a defender on the stick side.	To play a backhand overhead clear to rear tramlines from the back of the court.	To run 400m in 58 seconds.
❒ **Measurable**	10 repetitions.	Twenty repetitions.	Over 5 runs.
❒ **Accepted**	Yes.	Yes.	Yes.
❒ **Realistic**	60% success rate.	70% success rate.	80% success rate.
❒ **Time phased**	30 December.	1 August.	1 June.
❒ **Exciting**	Yes.	Yes.	Yes.
❒ **Recorded**	Performer and coach training diary.	Performer and coach training diary.	Performer and coach training diary.

Chapter 18 - MENTAL PREPARATION for SPORT PERFORMANCE - SELF-CONFIDENCE

Chapter 18 - MENTAL PREPARATION for SPORT PERFORMANCE - SELF-CONFIDENCE

SELF-CONFIDENCE

BANDURA'S SELF-EFFICACY THEORY

Self-efficacy was defined by Gould (1981) as: "**self-efficacy is a situation-specific form of self-confidence**".

- Bandura states that **self-efficacy predicts actual performance** when **skill and motivation are equal** (as between yourself and your opponent). If you are as motivated and skilful as your opponent whoever has the highest self-efficacy will win.

- According to Bandura **self-efficacy** can be **improved** by following his **4 component model**:

Self-Efficacy component	How to Improve Self-Efficacy
❒ **Performance accomplishments**	Highlight past good performances. This has the most powerful effect on self-efficacy.
❒ **Vicarious experiences**	Show the performer a demonstration of the required performance. This will persuade the performer that the task is achievable.
❒ **Verbal persuasion**	Verbally encourage the performer. Tell him / her that he / she has the ability to succeed.
❒ **Emotional arousal**	Get the performer to feel confident about his / her level of arousal and to alter the level of arousal to achieve the optimum level.

Chapter 18 - MENTAL PREPARATION for SPORT PERFORMANCE - SELF-CONFIDENCE

VEALEY'S MODEL OF SPORT CONFIDENCE

Vealey used **self-confidence** and **self-efficacy** theories in an attempt to develop a specific model of **confidence in sport**.

- **Sport confidence** is the **level of belief** a person has in his / her **ability to be successful at sport**.
- Success in sport can mean different things and could be related to **winning** (**outcome orientation**) or it could simply mean **performing well** (**performance orientation**). Vealey used the term **competitive orientation** to indicate whether a performer was **motivated** towards a **performance goal** or an **outcome goal**.
- According to Vealey the level of sport confidence can be assessed when the following factors are taken into account:
    - **Trait sport confidence** — The **level of sport confidence** a performer **usually** has.
    - **Competitive orientation** — The **perceived opportunity** to achieve a performance or outcome goal.
    - **State sport confidence** — The **level of sports confidence** a performer has in a **specific** sporting situation.
- **Trait sport confidence** and **competitive orientation** are used as predictors of how **confident a performer feels** in any sporting situation.
  For example, a footballer:
    - He / she will feel confident taking part in a penalty shoot out (**state sport confidence**).
    - If the performer is generally confident in his / her ability to take penalties (**trait sport confidence**).
    - If he / she is motivated by the opportunity to score the winning goal (**competitive orientation**).
- Vealey also related **attribution** theory to **sport confidence**. Performers' **attributions of success and failure** will have a direct **relationship** to **sport confidence**.
  For example, **attributing success** to factors such as **ability** and **effort** will **increase** a performer's **sport confidence** by **increasing** his / her **future expectancy of success**.
- The results from Vealey's work suggested that:
    - **Elite level performers** have **high levels of sport confidence**.
    - **Males** generally (in the broad population) tend to have **higher sport confidence** than **females**.
    - **Elite sporting males / females** show no **difference** in **sport confidence**.
    - This suggests that **elite female performers** are **less influenced** by **traditional gender roles**.
    - **Elite performers** also tended to be more **performance-orientated**, basing their feeling of competence on how **well they perform** rather than if they win or lose.

Chapter 18 - MENTAL PREPARATION for SPORT PERFORMANCE - SELF-CONFIDENCE

IMPLICATIONS FOR COACHES AND TEACHERS

- Coaches should **realise** that **performers** are individuals and have **different** levels of **trait confidence** and different **competitive orientations**. Improvement packages should be tailor-made to suit the **needs of the individual**.

- As **elite performers** tend to favour **performance goals**, **coaches** should try to set and emphasise **performance goals** at every level of performance.

- Use **attribution retraining** to increase the likelihood of the performer attributing success to factors that **increase the expectations of future success** thereby increasing sport confidence.

Chapter 19 - MENTAL PREPARATION for SPORT PERFORMANCE - CONCENTRATION

Chapter 19 - MENTAL PREPARATION for SPORT PERFORMANCE - CONCENTRATION

CONCENTRATION

This section is concerned with the performer's need to **attend to relevant cues** in order to use **selective attention** effectively. The **coach** needs to get the performer to **concentrate** on the **important information** and disregard the unimportant information. It is also important for **performers** to have the power to **concentrate for extended periods of time**.
For example, a test match cricketer or golfer.

NIDEFFER'S MODEL OF ATTENTIONAL STYLE

- Nideffer (1976) proposed that attention can be focused in **four ways**:
    - It could be focused **internally** on **thought or feelings**.
    - Or **externally** on **actions or events**.
    - It could be focused on a **narrow range** of **informational** cues.
    - Or could be focused on a **broad band** of **information**.

- An example of attentional focus relating to a Badminton player:
    - **Internal** "I need to think about using greater disguise on my short serve".
    - **External** Player concentrates on early detection of the shuttle in flight.
    - **Narrow** Player concentrates on wrist action when playing a smash.
    - **Broad** Player concentrates on every players' court position when playing doubles.

- Nideffer arranged the four types of **attentional focus** along **two dimensions** (or continua), **direction** and **width**. **Direction** ranged from **internal** to **external**, and **width** ranged from **narrow** to **broad**. In this way a performer could exhibit any one or two types of attentional focus.

Attentional focus	Used for	Example
Broad	Open skills.	Tacking in a yacht race.
Narrow	Closed skills.	Gymnastic vault.
Broad, Internal	Planning and analysing skills and tactics.	A football coach being overrun in midfield deciding whether to make substitutions and change team formation.
Broad, External	Decision making whilst playing.	A hockey player in front of goal assessing whether to shoot pass or dribble.
Narrow, External	Concentration on a target.	Archery or the early detection of the position of a cricket ball in the air.
Narrow, Internal	Mental rehearsal and thoughts concerning specific skills before and during events.	A full back psyching up before a rugby match, concentrating on fielding high kicks.

Chapter 19 - MENTAL PREPARATION for SPORT PERFORMANCE - CONCENTRATION

IMPROVING CONCENTRATION

Nideffer's model can be used to suggest ways in which **performance** can be **improved** through improvements in concentration or attentional focus. Performers need to know if they should be **focusing internally, externally, narrowly** or **broadly**. They need to be aware of **what** and **what not** to focus on, **when** to use a particular attentional focus and **how** to use it.

DEVELOPING ATTENTIONAL FOCUS

❒ In most sports, performers will need to learn **how to develop all four types of attentional focus.**
For example, the previous table showing attentional focus relating to a badminton player.

❒ Performers must be aware of the **type of attentional focus relevant** to a skill or activity. It has already been stated that a **broad focus** is most effective for **open skills**, whilst a **narrow focus** may be best for the performance of **closed skills.**

❒ **Problems** exist when performers **focus on the wrong information**. A player who has just given a penalty away may be focusing internally on his / her error when he / she should be using external and broad perspectives to focus on the game itself.

❒ An **inexperienced** games **player** can easily become **overloaded with information** whilst playing. The teacher or coach should highlight which information to concentrate on and which to ignore.

SELECTIVE ATTENTION

❒ Performers need to be taught **how to use selective attention**. Whatever the focus of attention, a performer's **attentional capacity is limited**. It is important that the performer **selectively attends** to the **correct information** and **disregards** the **unimportant information.**

❒ A player must be able to **selectively attend** to **internal** and **external information.**

❒ Make sure that a performer's **personal thoughts** about performance are related to **positive outcomes**. **Negative** thought can be damaging and result in a **loss of confidence.**

Chapter 19 - MENTAL PREPARATION for SPORT PERFORMANCE - CONCENTRATION

IMPROVING CONCENTRATION (continued)

DISTRACTION

- **Distraction should be avoided**. A **lapse in concentration** can be **disastrous** to any sports player. Performers can prepare themselves for possible **distractions** during competition by **practising in distracting circumstances**.

- Coaches can deliberately try to distract performers (in training) by playing music or taped crowd noises. Performers can practice against opponents who cheat, frustrate, call out and by any method attempt to distract them.

SWITCHING / BROADENING ATTENTIONAL FOCUS

- Performers need to be able to **switch their attentional focus**.
  For example, a goal keeper will need to have a **broad external focus** to assess the situation in front of goal.
  - He / she will need to **narrow the attentional focus** to concentrate on an attacker shooting and then making a save.
  - He / she will then need to **broaden** his / her **attentional focus** in order to distribute the ball effectively (supposing that the ball was gathered from the shot).

- Problems exist if a performer **cannot switch attentional focus**.
  For example, the games player faced with a one-verses-one situation decides to take on the player.
  - He / she probably would have passed to the team mate who was "free" if he / she had looked up rather than concentrating on the defender.

CONTROL OF AROUSAL

- According to **Easterbrook's Cue Utilisation Theory**, increasing **arousal levels** lead to a **narrowing** of **attentional focus**.

- This explains why some performers are said to have "**tunnel vision**". A **highly aroused** games player can often make a **wrong decision** if he / she **cannot broaden** his / her **attentional focus**.
  For example, a team's play maker needs to have a broad focus of attention in order to pick out free players and make appropriate passes.
  - If his / her focus is narrowed the entire team's performance can suffer.

- Whilst trying to improve personal concentration, **try to disrupt** opponents' concentration. Use **distraction tactics**, use **disguise**, try to "wind-up" an opponent.

Chapter 20 - MENTAL PREPARATION for SPORT PERFORMANCE - EMOTIONAL CONTROL

Chapter 20 - MENTAL PREPARATION for SPORT PERFORMANCE - EMOTIONAL CONTROL

EMOTIONAL CONTROL

Optimum performance occurs when the performer attains a **particular state of arousal**. **Too little arousal** and the performer can find it **difficult to focus** and concentrate on relevant cues. **Too much arousal** and the performer can become **tense**, **anxious** and **lose attentional focus**.

- The most **effective level of arousal** depends on the **personality** of the performer, the **type of task**, and the **level of learning** of the performer. The most effective **coach** is one who can **manipulate** the performer's **level of arousal** to best suit the person and the task.
  - **Arousal** The state of **activation** or excitement a person has in any situation.
  - **Anxiety** A **negative reaction to stress** resulting in over-arousal.
  - **Excitement** A **positive reaction to stress**.
  - **Stress** A **stimulus resulting in arousal** or a response to a situation.

ANXIETY

- **Anxiety** is a **negative physiological and emotional response to stress**.
- **Anxiety** is multidimensional having both **cognitive** and **somatic components**.

Cognitive Anxiety (Emotional Feelings)

- Alert.
- Awake.
- Scared.
- Apprehensive.
- Negative thoughts.

Somatic Anxiety (Physiological signs)

- Increased muscle tension.
- High respiration rate.
- High heart rate.
- Increased perspiration.
- Relaxation of smooth muscle.

- **Anxiety** results in **over-arousal**.
- **Anxiety** levels can vary over time and can **vary in intensity**.
  - **State anxiety** A person's immediate emotional state in any one situation.
  - **Trait anxiety** A person's **general** proneness to anxiety, his / her general arousal level.
- **Anxiety** is a **response to stress**. **Stress** is perceived as **threatening** and results in the body being made ready for the **Fight or Flight response**. The **threat** can either be the **threat of injury** or **ego threat**.

Chapter 20 - MENTAL PREPARATION for SPORT PERFORMANCE - EMOTIONAL CONTROL

STRESS

- The word **stress** has often been used to **mean anxiety**. More recently its meaning has slightly altered.
    - Anxiety is **over-arousal** which results in a **decrease in performance**.
    - **Stress** describes the **conditions** that lead a person to **become anxious**.
    - **Stress** can be both **beneficial or harmful**.

STRESSORS

- **Stressors** are **environmental conditions that cause stress**.
  Examples of **stressors** are:
    - **Competition** Competition naturally increases arousal levels and causes stress.
    - **Frustration** Being prevented from achieving a goal.
    - **Climate** Both hot and cold climates can be stressful.

- **Stress** can be **beneficial** because it **energises the performer** into trying his / her hardest.

- Some people **seek out stressful experiences** because of the extreme feelings that can be gained. These feelings are known as **eustress**. These feelings are those sought by people participating in hazardous activities like parachuting and bungy jumping.

- **Stress** can be **negative** when the performer becomes **overaroused**. The performer then becomes **tense**, **anxious**, can suffer a **loss in concentration** and is more likely to **make a mistake**.

Chapter 20 - MENTAL PREPARATION for SPORT PERFORMANCE - EMOTIONAL CONTROL

THE RELATIONSHIP BETWEEN AROUSAL AND PERFORMANCE

THE INVERTED 'U' THEORY

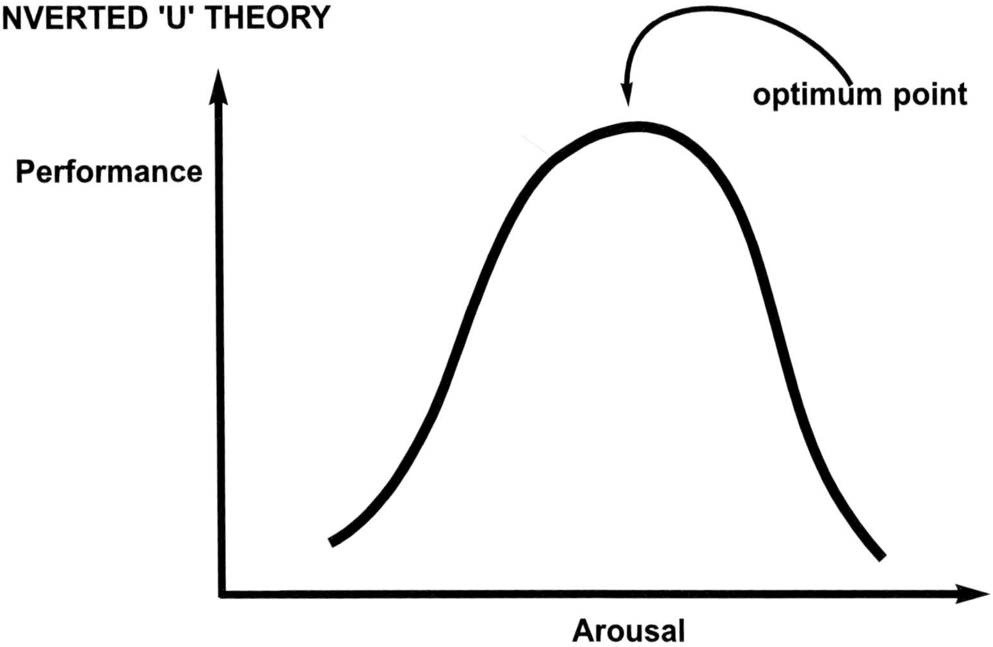

In this theory:

- **Performance increases** with increasing levels of **arousal** up to a point (the **optimum** point). After this point, **increasing** levels of **arousal** bring about **decreasing** levels of performance.

- The **optimum point** marks out the most beneficial level of arousal for any task. It can change depending on the **task**, level of **learning** and **personality** of the performer.

- The coach will try to arouse but not over-arouse the athlete, who will then be at the optimum point.

Chapter 20 - MENTAL PREPARATION for SPORT PERFORMANCE - EMOTIONAL CONTROL

HULL'S DRIVE THEORY

This is an alternative to the Inverted 'U' theory.

- **Drive** refers to the **level of arousal** possessed by a performer. Drive Theory states that **performance increases** with **increasing** levels of **arousal**. The more arousal the better the performance. However, Hull added that this would only be the case if the **skill** had previously been **well-learned**.

- Performance levels for a **beginner** would **reduce** with increasing levels of arousal. This theory explains why, for many beginners, it is easy to perform a skill when there is no pressure, but when pressure is introduced, mistakes start to be made.

- Alternatively an increase in pressure can actually help the **skilled athlete** perform to the **best** of his / her ability.

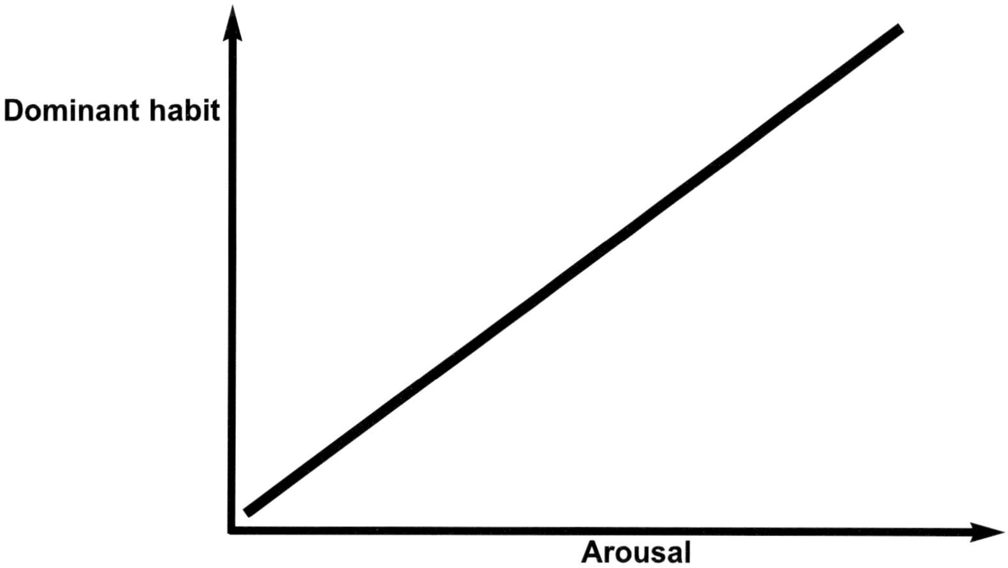

According to **Hull's** Drive theory: **Performance = Habit x Drive**

- **Habit** refers to the **strength of the learned response** or skill, and whether the **correct response** has been practised until it has become habitualised. Any response can have a strong or weak habit depending on the **level of practice** at that skill. **Drive** refers to the **level of arousal** of the performer.

- **Increased levels** of arousal are said to bring about the **dominant response** (strongest from a number of possibilities).

- For the **novice** the dominant response is usually **incorrect** due to a **low level** of habit (movements are poorly-learned and full of mistakes). For the **experienced performer**, the dominant response is usually **correct** due to the skill becoming well-learned and therefore habitualised.

- Until a **skill** has been **well-learned**, any increase in arousal will probably result in a decrease in performance. Once a skill is **fully-learned**, increased arousal is more likely to cause increased performance.

Chapter 20 - MENTAL PREPARATION for SPORT PERFORMANCE - EMOTIONAL CONTROL

OPTIMUM LEVELS OF AROUSAL

The optimum level of arousal is dependent on a number of factors including **task difficulty, type of task, level of learning** and **personality**.

- For **simple** skills, the learner will need to be **more aroused** than for **complex** skills. If the task is **simple** it is easy for the performer to become disinterested. Higher levels of arousal will ensure greater concentration.
- **Complex** skills require large amounts of **attentional capacity** and so need lower levels of arousal. **Excessive arousal** can cause frustration and narrowing of attentional focus (tunnel vision). This can be detrimental to performance.
- **High** levels of **arousal** for **fine motor skills** such as those found in snooker, can be **detrimental** to performance due to unwanted increases in muscle tension.
- **Gross motor skills** such as those found in weight lifting, need relatively higher levels of arousal than for fine motor skills.
- **Hazardous** activities will require high levels of arousal.
- At the **early stages of learning**, arousal levels need to be relatively low. **Too much arousal** can affect the learner's ability to attend to information. At **later stages of learning** when the learner has spare attentional capacity, greater levels of arousal can help motivate the performer.
- **Personality** can affect optimum arousal levels. The **introvert** may find it easy to become **over-aroused** whilst the **extrovert** will **need increased** levels of **arousal** to reach the optimum point. If the performer requires greater levels of arousal to reach the optimum point, then the inverted 'U' curve is shifted to the right as illustrated below.

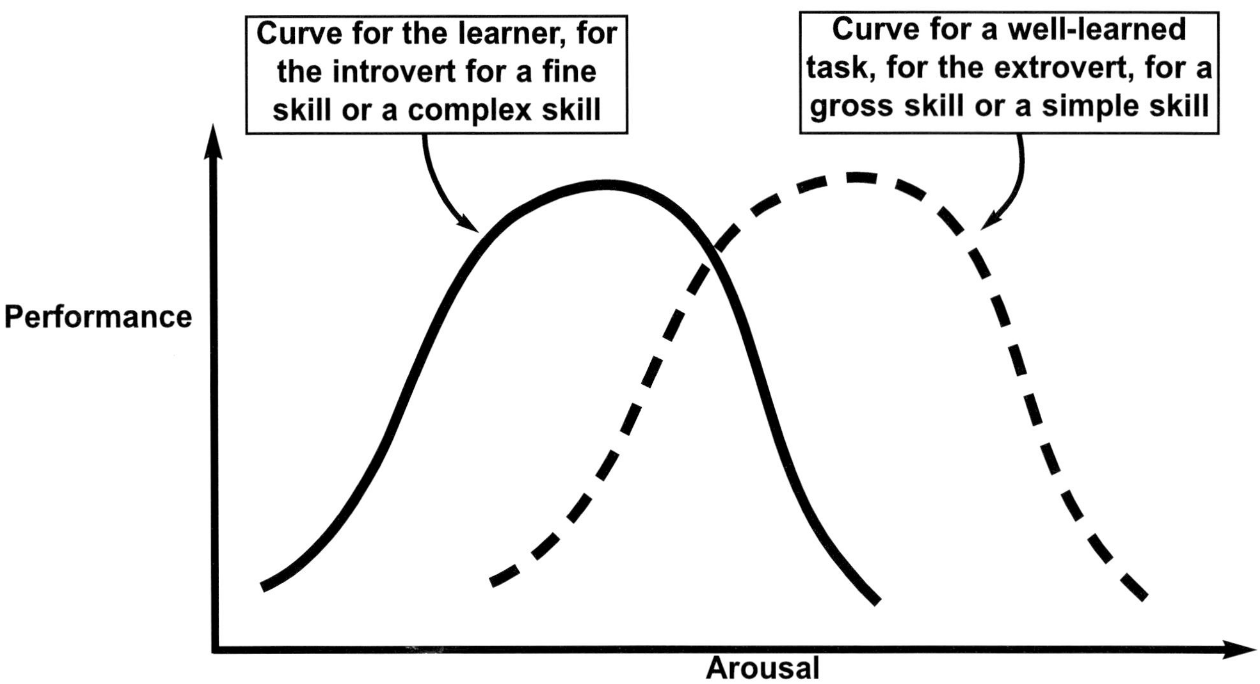

Chapter 20 - MENTAL PREPARATION for SPORT PERFORMANCE - EMOTIONAL CONTROL

AROUSAL THEORIES

HANIN'S ZONE OF OPTIMUM FUNCTIONING (1997)

Hanin adapted **Inverted 'U' Theory** when working with Russian athletes in the 1980's. His work **differed** from Inverted 'U' Theory in **two ways**:

- The **optimal level of performance** does **not** always have to be at a **mid-point** between low and high levels of arousal.
- The **optimal level of performance** is not a single point but rather **a band or zone**.

- According to Hanin, an athlete's **best performance** can be obtained in a **zone** which may be of low, medium or high arousal.
- **Different athletes** will respond **differently** to the **same arousal situations**. Hence **optimum performances** are an individual function of **personality**, **type of skill** and **degree of habit** (the strength and permanence of a correctly learned skill).

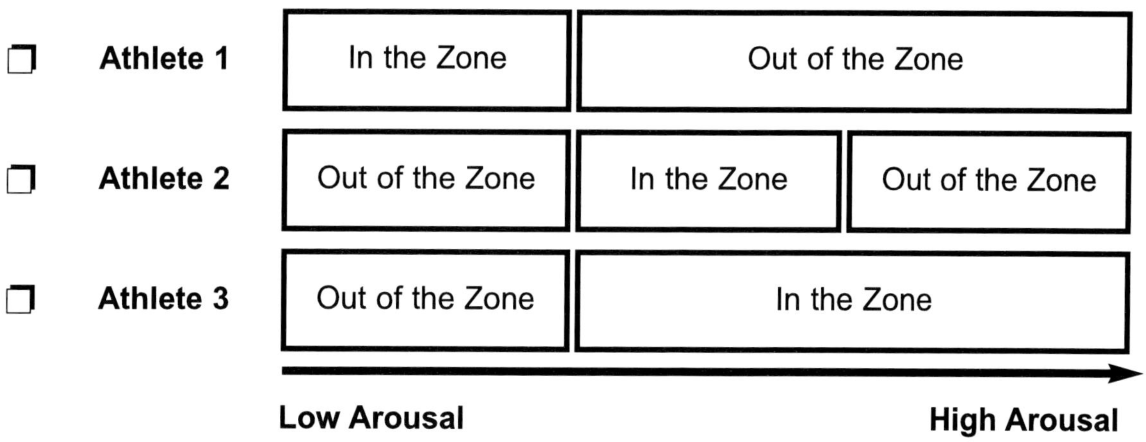

Chapter 20 - MENTAL PREPARATION for SPORT PERFORMANCE - EMOTIONAL CONTROL

CSIKZENTMIHALYI'S PEAK FLOW THEORY

According to **Csikzentmihalyi** (1990), **flow** is an **optimal experience** that is **intrinsically rewarding**. The term **flow** describes a period of **peak performance** when the performer feels **totally involved**. The performer feels that he / she can achieve at the highest level without effort - without having to concentrate on any particular element of the performance. To understand more about flow we need to discover how flow can occur and how to get the performer in a state of **peak flow**.

- **Peak flow** is likely to occur in the following ways:
  - When **task demands match the skill level** of the performer.
  - When **actions** and **reactions** become **automatic**.
  - When **concentration** is total.
  - When the **performer** feels **in control** without having to exert control.
  - When the **performer loses self-consciousness**.
  - When **time** appears to **slow down** or **speed up**.
  - When the **performer** finds **activity** extremely **rewarding**.

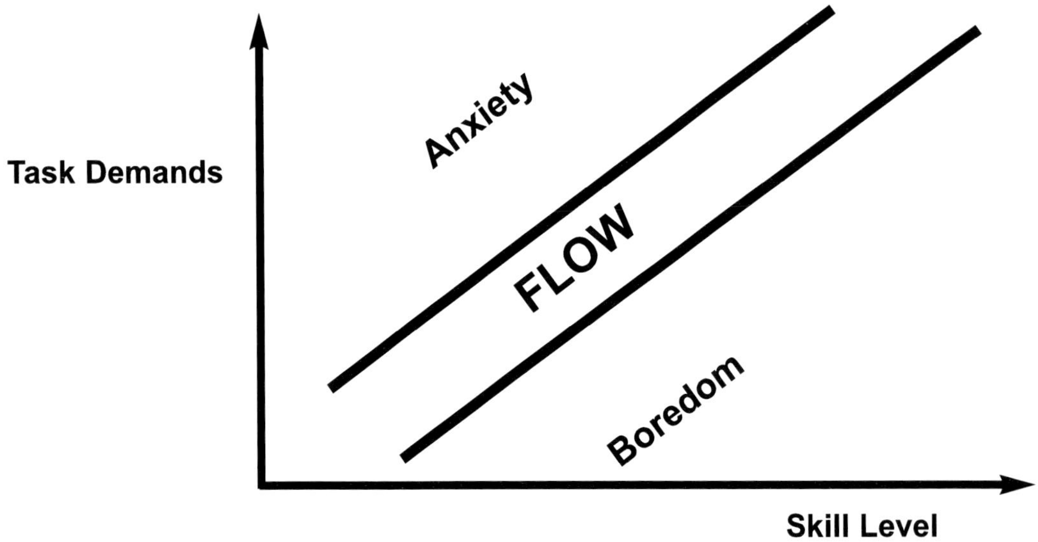

- The graph shows that the **flow state** is achieved when **skill levels are equivalent to task demands**. If **skill levels exceed task demands** the performer would find the challenge **boring**. If **task demands exceed skill levels** the performer would become **frustrated** and **anxious**.

- It is the **role of the coach** to try and **match skill levels and task demands** in order for the performer to **achieve peak flow**. **Problems** exist when a performer allows **negative thoughts** (or **anxiety** or being **distracted**) to disrupt the flow state.

- Jackson (1992) has suggested **four ways** that a performer can attempt to attain and remain in the flow experience:
  - **Positive mental attitude** — "I can do it."
  - **Control anxiety** — Stay relaxed, enjoy yourself.
  - **Maintain focus** — Maintain concentration and remain confident.
  - **Physical readiness** — Keep at the peak of fitness.

Chapter 20 - MENTAL PREPARATION for SPORT PERFORMANCE - EMOTIONAL CONTROL

MULTIDIMENSIONAL MODELS

It has already been shown that **arousal has two forms**, a psychological or **cognitive** form and a physiological or **somatic** form. **Arousal** is therefore viewed as having **more than one dimension**; arousal is multidimensional.

- According to **multidimensional anxiety theory**, an **increase in cognitive** as opposed to **somatic** arousal may bring about **different changes in performance**.

- The relationship between **somatic arousal** and **performance** is said to follow the curve of the **Inverted 'U'**, whilst the relationship between **cognitive arousal** and **performance is different**. A rise in cognitive arousal is said to bring about a **decrease in performance**.

- A rise in **cognitive arousal** is supposed to increase the chance of a performer **worrying** about performance, giving rise to **apprehension**, **doubts** and **negative thoughts**. This in turn may lead to a performer "**choking**" in a **pressurised** situation.
  For example, the tennis player who double faults on an important point.

REVERSAL THEORY

According to **Reversal Theory**, it is not arousal levels that cause problems with performance but how the performer **perceives** the arousal.

- **High arousal** could be perceived as being **positive** (exciting) **or negative** (frightening) or **both**.
  For example, skiing a black run.

- According to **Martens** (1997) if a person **interprets arousal positively**, **performance** will be **positively** affected.

- If a person **interprets arousal negatively**, **performance** will be **negatively** affected. Consequently coaches should try to make performers view situations as **challenging opportunities** rather than frightening propositions.

Chapter 20 - MENTAL PREPARATION for SPORT PERFORMANCE - EMOTIONAL CONTROL

CATASTROPHE THEORY

One way of understanding the influence of cognitive arousal is through **Catastrophe Theory**.

- Hardy (1990) proposed the idea that when a performer has a **high level of cognitive arousal**, an **increase in somatic arousal** above a certain point (the **maximum arousal point**) could lead to a **catastrophic decrease in performance**.

  For example, the Rugby player who gets so psyched up that he spends the first ten minutes of the game chasing targets and giving away penalties.
  The coach would need to substitute the player until his arousal level has dropped enough for it not to impair performance.

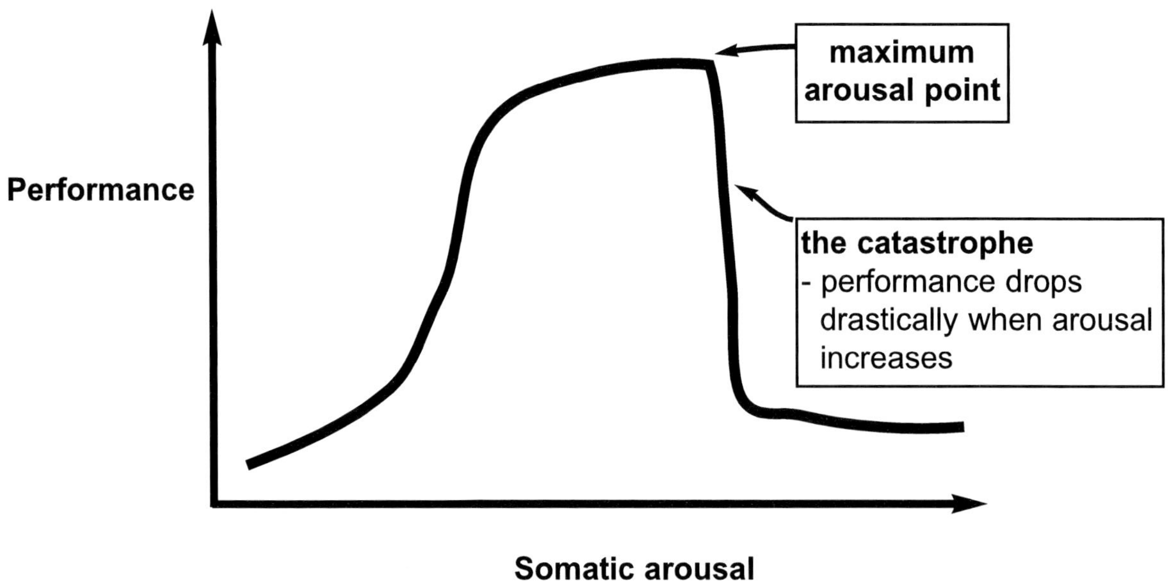

Chapter 20 - MENTAL PREPARATION for SPORT PERFORMANCE - EMOTIONAL CONTROL

THE SIGNIFICANCE OF AROUSAL THEORIES

The following statements are a summary of arousal theories and the **relationship between arousal and performance**.

- **Performers function best at a particular arousal level or band of arousal.**
  - According to **Inverted 'U' Theory optimum performance** occurs at **moderate levels of arousal**.
  - Alternatively, **Hanin** argues that **optimum performance** can occur at **low**, **moderate** or **high** levels of **arousal** depending on the indiviual performer, and that **optimal performance** occurs within an **arousal band** rather than a point of arousal.

- **Arousal is multidimensional.**
  - **Arousal** is said to be **multidimensional** because it has a number of different parts. **Coaches** and teachers need to consider **cognitive arousal** (psychological) and **somatic** (physiological) **arousal**.

- **The relationship between anxiety and performance depends on the way the anxiety is perceived by the performer.**
  - According to **reversal theory** the affect of arousal on performance depends on how the **performer perceives increased arousal**.

    For example, a shot putter who experiences an increased heart rate and butterflies in the stomach could interpret those feelings as nerves and get **worried**. Alternatively the shot putter may believe that the feelings show her that her body is ready to perform and that she is **excited** rather than frightened.

- **Optimum levels of arousal can vary depending on personality, level of learning and type of task.**

- **Over-arousal can lead to dramatic decreases in performance (Catastrophe theory).**

- **Optimal performance occurs when task demands match a performer's skill level (Peak Flow theory).**

Chapter 20 - MENTAL PREPARATION for SPORT PERFORMANCE - EMOTIONAL CONTROL

THE DETRIMENTAL EFFECTS OF AROUSAL ON PERFORMANCE AND HOW TO COMBAT THEM

- **Low levels of arousal can result in a broad attentional focus and constant attentional switching**.
    - This is **detrimental to performance** because of a **reduction** in the performer's ability to **maintain concentration**. **Coaches** and teachers need to ensure that performers are **correctly focused** by **increasing arousal levels accordingly**.

- **Low levels of arousal do not prepare the body for strenuous exercise**.
    - In order to perform **active sports** the body needs an **increased blood supply** to the working muscles. **At low levels of arousal the body is not adequately prepared** for sudden bursts of activity.
    - Performers need to undertake a **psychological** as well as physiological **warm-up** before competing. This provides **mental preparation** for the subsequent performance.

- **High arousal leads to an increase in muscular tension which can lead to coordination difficulties for the performer**.
    - In **sports requiring fine motor skills**, such as putting in golf, the performer needs a **light accurate touch**. An increase in **muscular tension** can lead to a putt being over-hit.
    - In order to combat the effects of increased somatic arousal, performers need to learn **somatic management techniques**, such as progressive muscular relaxation and biofeedback.

- **High arousal leads to changes in attentional focus, specifically a narrowing of attentional focus causing "tunnel vision"**.
    - This would cause **problems** to any sports player who needs a **broad focus of attention**.
      For example, the rugby fly-half who needs to assess a broad range of environmental information before deciding to run, pass or kick.
    - The **coach** or teacher can use **Attentional Control Training** (**ACT**) as a way of providing a **personalised programme** to target a performer's **specific concentration problems**. **ACT** assesses the **demands** of the sport, the **situation** and the **personality** of the performer in order to provide a tailor-made programme.

- **High arousal levels bring about an increased likelihood of the performer experiencing negative thoughts**.
    - This in turn can result in a performer "**choking**" at important moments due to **negative thoughts** affecting the performer's **confidence**. In order to combat the effects of **increased cognitive arousal**, performers need to learn **cognitive management techniques** such as **positive thinking**, **thought stopping** and **mental rehearsal**.

Chapter 20 - MENTAL PREPARATION for SPORT PERFORMANCE - EMOTIONAL CONTROL

THE MANAGEMENT OF ANXIETY

COGNITIVE TECHNIQUES

Cognitive techniques help the performer to **reduce worry** and **negative thoughts** by thinking about the task.

- **Thought stopping** — When the performer feels a **negative thought** he / she should immediately think "**STOP**" and **substitute a positive thought**.
- **Imagery** — The performer **imagines** him / herself in a **calm peaceful setting** where he / she is in control.
- **Directing attention** — The performer **directs** his / her **attention** on particular aspects of performance thereby **avoiding negative thought**.
- **Mental Rehearsal** — This is a form of **imagery**. It can also be used to **practise overcoming negative thoughts** or situations which give rise to negative thoughts.
  - **Internal mental rehearsal** involves imagining how the movement **felt**.
  - **External mental rehearsal** involves imagining the **sporting environment**.
  - **Mental rehearsal** is performed in the following way:
    - **Relax** the athlete.
    - **Identify the skill** to be rehearsed.
    - **Identify key points** of the skill.
    - **Imagine** and **focus** on the key points.
    - Imagine as **vividly as possible**.
    - Devise a **mnemonic** to remember the key points.
    - **Practise**.

SOMATIC TECHNIQUES

- **Slow deep breathing reduces respiration rate** and can help reduce **heart rate**.
- **Progressive relaxation** (Jacobson 1938) involves the tensing and then relaxing of various muscle groups.
  - The effect is to **super-relax** the muscles. Initially sessions may take 45-60 minutes but with practice the effect can take a lot less time.
  - The aim is for performers to **recognise increased muscular tension** and **relax the muscles at will**.
    For example, the tennis player about to serve notices tension in the shoulder and arm and focuses attention on relaxing those muscles.
- **Meditation** can relax the mind. It is assumed that a **relaxed mind** will help to **relax the body**.
- **Biofeedback** gives the performer immediate physiological feedback.
  - For example, heart and respiration rates. The performer then **tries to reduce** any of the physiological parameters being measured. He / she will receive **immediate feedback** relating to the **success** of his / her efforts.
  - The easiest method of obtaining biofeedback is by **recording skin temperature**. **Increased arousal levels** result in a **decrease in skin temperature** of the extremities. When a subject is made aware of a decrease in temperature he / she tries to increase his / her temperature.

Chapter 20 - MENTAL PREPARATION for SPORT PERFORMANCE - EMOTIONAL CONTROL

THE MEASUREMENT OF ANXIETY OR STRESS

SELF-REPORT QUESTIONNAIRES

These are simple to administer but **subjects may lie**.

Marten's Sport Competitive Anxiety Test (SCAT)

- Measures the emotional and physiological responses to stress in the competitive environment.
- The results are given as a percentile of the population.
  For example, if a person scored in the 75th percentile then 25% of the population would have a have higher competitive anxiety.

- See an example of a student version of **SCAT** on page 180, Appendix 6 below.

Marten's Competitive State Anxiety Inventory (CSAI)

- One of the only measures to include self-confidence.

Speilberger's State, Trait Anxiety Inventory (STAI)

- Measures the emotional and physiological responses to stress in general and specific situations.

- See an example of a student version of **STAI** on page 181, Appendix 7 below.

Smith's Sport Anxiety Scale (SAS)

- A multidimensional model including two cognitive anxiety scales and one somatic anxiety scale.

PHYSIOLOGICAL MEASURES

These produce **reliable results** but are **expensive** to administer.

- **The Galvanic Skin Response**: measures **skin conductivity**.
- **Sudorimeter**: measures **sweating**.
- **Electrocardiogram (ECG)**: measures **heart rate**.
- **Electromyogram (EMG)**: measures **muscle tension**.
- **Electroencephalogram (EEG)**: measures **brain wave activity**.

BEHAVIOURAL MEASURES

Involve **observing the performance** of sports players. This method is **subjective**.

Section 3 - Appendices

Section 3 - Appendix 1 - Attitude Towards Physical Activity Questionnaire

STUDENT ATTITUDE TO PHYSICAL ACTIVITY QUESTIONNAIRE

(after Biddle S.J. 1996)

Physical Activity in the context of this questionnaire means exercise:

- ❒ Which is suitably **vigorous**.
- ❒ For at least **20 minutes** per day within a **game** or **individual sporting activity**.
- ❒ Which causes **heart rate** to increase to at least **120 beats per minute** at some time during the activity.
- ❒ Or which causes you to be out of breath either during or immediately after the activity.

- ❒ There are no right or wrong answers to the questions: attempt the questionnaire quickly, then calculate your score:

  - ❒ **You have problems as a sportsperson if your score is less than 27!**

1) **If I take part in vigorous exercise at least 4 times per week for 6 weeks, this would be good for my health**:
1 - very unlikely 2 - unlikely 3 - perhaps 4 - yes 5 - very good

2) **If I take part in moderate exercise every day for 1 month this would reduce tension**:
1 - very unlikely 2 - unlikely 3 - perhaps 4 - yes 5 - very much

3) **If I take part in vigorous exercise regularly this would enable me to socialise with my friends**:
1 - very unlikely 2 - unlikely 3 - perhaps 4 - yes 5 - very much

4) **How many times in a week on average do you take part in moderate or vigorous exercise?**
1 - zero 2 - once 3 - twice 4 - three times 5 - four or more

5) **If I take part in vigorous exercise regularly this would be a good thing**:
1 - not likely 2 - disagree 3 - perhaps 4 - yes 5 - very much

6) **Being healthy and fit is**:
1 - very bad 2 - bad 3 - OK 4 - good 5 - very good

7) **Reducing tension and anger is**:
1 - very bad 2 - bad 3 - OK 4 - good 5 - very good

8) **Being able to socialise with my friends during exercise is**:
1 - very bad 2 - bad 3 - OK 4 - good 5 - very good

9) **I intend to take part in vigorous exercise regularly over the next 6 weeks**:
1 - not likely 2 - no 3 - perhaps 4 - yes 5 - very much

Name :______________________________ **Score :**________________

Section 3 - Appendix 2 - Achievement Motivation Questionnaire

STUDENT ACHIEVEMENT MOTIVATION QUESTIONNAIRE

(after Lynn - see Carron A.V. 1980)

1)	**Are you happy to be friendly with someone who is careless and disorganised?**	no yes	- 1 - 0
2)	**Are you happy if food is wasted at a meal?**	no yes	- 1 - 0
3)	**Are you happy to work with someone who is friendly but incompetent rather than someone who is capable but difficult to be with?**	no yes	- 1 - 0
4)	**Are you able to completely forget your work when on holiday?**	no yes	- 1 - 0
5)	**Have you always worked hard to be the best at your sport?**	yes no	- 1 - 0
6)	**Are you happy to be late for lectures or classes?**	yes no	- 1 - 0
7)	**Do you enjoy taking too much alcohol?**	no yes	- 1 - 0
8)	**Do you get angry if one of your friends is late for an important activity?**	yes no	- 1 - 0

Add up the total score - a score of zero would indicate a very low achievement motivation.

Name:____________________________ **Score:**____________________

Section 3 - Appendix 3 - Attribution Questionnaire

STUDENT ATTRIBUTION QUESTIONNAIRE

(after Weiner, see Carron A.V. 1980)

A) Imagine a winning experience in your sport - one that you can strongly link with success and a good feeling about your sport.

1) How much do you feel that your OWN ABILITY was an important part of the success?
1 - not at all 2 - not much 3 - perhaps 4 - a little 5 - very much so

2) How much do you feel that your OPPONENT'S LACK OF ABILITY was an important part of the success?
1 - not at all 2 - not much 3 - perhaps 4 - a little 5 - very much so

3) How much do you feel that your GOOD LUCK was an important part of the success?
1 - not at all 2 - not much 3 - perhaps 4 - a little 5 - very much so

4) How much do you feel that your OWN HIGH EFFORT was an important part of the success?
1 - not at all 2 - not much 3 - perhaps 4 - a little 5 - very much so

B) Imagine a losing or very poor experience in your sport - one that you can strongly link with failure and a bad feeling about your sport.

1) How much do you feel that your OWN LACK OF ABILITY was an important part of the failure?
1 - not at all 2 - not much 3 - perhaps 4 - a little 5 - very much so

2) How much do you feel that your OPPONENT'S HIGH ABILITY was an important part of the failure?
1 - not at all 2 - not much 3 - perhaps 4 - a little 5 - very much so

3) How much do you feel that your BAD LUCK was an important part of the failure?
1 - not at all 2 - not much 3 - perhaps 4 - a little 5 - very much so

4) How much do you feel that your OWN LACK OF EFFORT was an important part of the failure?
1 - not at all 2 - not much 3 - perhaps 4 - a little 5 - very much so

- ❐ **Now enter your attribution scores for both success and failure in the score chart on the next page.**
- ❐ **It would be helpful to record ALL scores for your group on the chart.**
- ❐ **Calculate the average score for the group for each of the attribution factors.**

Section 3 - Appendix 3 - Attribution Questionnaire

SCORE CHART FOR ATTRIBUTION QUESTIONNAIRE

Name:______________________________ Initial Assessment / Average Scores

		Locus of Causality	
		INTERNAL	EXTERNAL
Stability	STABLE	Ability	Task Difficulty
	UNSTABLE	Effort	Luck

Section 3 - Appendix 4 - The Leadership Scale for Sport (LSS)

STUDENT LEADERSHIP SCALE FOR SPORT (LSS)

(after Chelladurai)

Mark the score for each of the following statements according to HOW YOU FEEL about the issue - NOT what you think ought to be the case.

1) As a sportsperson, I prefer my coach to emphasise hard, vigorous training to improve my standard of performance: (Training and Instruction Behaviour)

1 - not at all 2 - not much 3 - hardly 4 - perhaps 5 - a little 6 - usually 7 - always

2) As a sportsperson, I prefer my coach to make all the decisions: (Autocratic Behaviour)

1 - not at all 2 - not much 3 - hardly 4 - perhaps 5 - a little 6 - usually 7 - always

3) As a sportsperson, I prefer my coach to allow the group a say in deciding team aims and goals, a say in which activities should be done, and a say in which tactics and strategies should be used: (Democratic Behaviour)

1 - not at all 2 - not much 3 - hardly 4 - perhaps 5 - a little 6 - usually 7 - always

4) As a sportsperson, I prefer my coach to be concerned about individual sportspersons and their wishes and feelings, to enable a positive group atmosphere to develop: (Social Support Behaviour)

1 - not at all 2 - not much 3 - hardly 4 - perhaps 5 - a little 6 - usually 7 - always

5) As a sportsperson, I prefer my coach to recognise good personal results using praise as reward: (Rewarding Behaviour)

1 - not at all 2 - not much 3 - hardly 4 - perhaps 5 - a little 6 - usually 7 - always

Decide from the scores which leadership style you prefer most.

Name: ________________________________

Most Preferred Leadership Style: ____

Section 3 - Appendix 5 - The Least Preferred Coworker Scale (LPC)

STUDENT LEAST PREFERED COWORKER SCALE (LPC)

(after Fiedler)

- ❒ Think about the **PERSON YOU WOULD LEAST LIKE TO WORK WITH**.
- ❒ Mark the score for each of the following attributes of the person according to **HOW YOU FEEL about this person**.
- ❒ Note that this person does not have to be an enemy or someone you don't get on with - but someone whose work habits you find great difficulty in cooperating with.

Pleasant	8	7	6	5	4	3	2	1	**Unpleasant**
Friendly	8	7	6	5	4	3	2	1	**Unfriendly**
Rejecting	1	2	3	4	5	6	7	8	**Accepting**
Helpful	8	7	6	5	4	3	2	1	**Frustrating**
Unenthusiastic	1	2	3	4	5	6	7	8	**Enthusiastic**
Tense	1	2	3	4	5	6	7	8	**Relaxed**
Distant	1	2	3	4	5	6	7	8	**Close**
Cold	1	2	3	4	5	6	7	8	**Warm**
Cooperative	8	7	6	5	4	3	2	1	**Uncooperative**
Supportive	8	7	6	5	4	3	2	1	**Hostile**
Boring	1	2	3	4	5	6	7	8	**Interesting**
Quarrelsome	1	2	3	4	5	6	7	8	**Harmonious**
Self Assured	8	7	6	5	4	3	2	1	**Hesitant**
Efficient	8	7	6	5	4	3	2	1	**Inefficient**
Gloomy	1	2	3	4	5	6	7	8	**Cheerful**
Open	8	7	6	5	4	3	2	1	**Guarded**

- ❒ **Now add up the scores and divide by 16 to obtain your mean score.**

Name:______________________________

- ❒ **Total score =**________________________ **Mean score =**___________________________

- ❒ **A mean of less than 4.5 implies that your LPC is a task-oriented leader type.**
- ❒ **A mean of more than 4.5 implies that your LPC is a person-oriented leader type.**

Section 3 - Appendix 6 - The Sport Competitive Anxiety Test (SCAT)

STUDENT SPORT COMPETITIVE ANXIETY TEST (after Martens)

- Look below at the list of statements about **how you might feel** when facing a sporting **competitive situation.**
- You have to decide whether you **HARDLY EVER, SOMETIMES or OFTEN** experience the feelings mentioned.
- Don't spend too much time on each statement - respond **honestly** and **quickly** by ringing the chosen answer on the sheet.
- There is **no right or wrong answer** to each statement.
- Remember to choose the answer you **USUALLY** feel.

1) Individual sports are more exciting than team sports:	hardly ever	sometimes	often
2) Before I compete I get a nauseous feeling in my stomach:	hardly ever	sometimes	often
3) When I compete I am concerned about making mistakes:	hardly ever	sometimes	often
4) Setting a goal is important when competing:	hardly ever	sometimes	often
5) When I compete I am a poor loser:	hardly ever	sometimes	often
6) Before I compete I am nervous:	hardly ever	sometimes	often
7) Just before competing my heart rate increases:	hardly ever	sometimes	often
8) Before I compete I am uncomfortable:	hardly ever	sometimes	often
9) Before I compete I am uptight:	hardly ever	sometimes	often
10) I enjoy the social side of competitions:	hardly ever	sometimes	often
11) Before I compete I am relaxed and confident:	hardly ever	sometimes	often
12) Waiting to compete is the worst part of the sport:	hardly ever	sometimes	often
13) I most enjoy sports which don't require a lot of effort:	hardly ever	sometimes	often
14) Before I compete I am calm:	hardly ever	sometimes	often
15) Before I compete I worry about not performing well:	hardly ever	sometimes	often

- **Scoring for questions 2, 3, 6, 7, 8, 9, 12, 15 is as follows:**
  hardly ever - 1 sometimes - 2 often - 3
- **Scoring for questions 11, 14, is as follows:**
  hardly ever - 3 sometimes - 2 often - 1
- **Questions 1, 4, 5, 10, 13, are not scored.**

- **Mark your scores on the sheet, add them up and draw a conclusion about your anxiety state when competing.**

- **Name:____________________________ SCAT score:_________________**

Section 3 - Appendix 7 - The State Trait Anxiety Inventory (STAI)

STUDENT STATE TRAIT ANXIETY INVENTORY (after Speilberger)

- Look below at the list of statements about **how you might describe yourself**.
- You have to decide whether you **ALMOST NEVER, SOMETIMES or OFTEN** can apply the statement to you or your feelings about yourself.
- Don't spend too much time on each statement - respond **honestly and quickly** by ringing the chosen answer on the sheet.
- There is **no right or wrong answer** to each statement.
- Remember to choose the answer you **USUALLY** feel.

1) I am calm cool and collected:	almost never	sometimes	often
2) I tire easily:	almost never	sometimes	often
3) Other people always seem happier than I am:	almost never	sometimes	often
4) I often feel depressed when things don't go my way:	almost never	sometimes	often
5) I feel comfortable:	almost never	sometimes	often
6) I feel tense or angry about things that have happened recently:	almost never	sometimes	often
7) I feel secure:	almost never	sometimes	often
8) Small things which happen to me give me great concern:	almost never	sometimes	often

- **Score questions 1, 5, 7 as follows: almost never - 3 sometimes - 2 often - 1**
- **Score questions 2, 3, 4, 6, 8 as follows: almost never - 1 sometimes - 2 often - 3**

- **Name:________________________________ STAI score:_________________**

- **Does this score indicate a high or low trait anxiety level in yourself?**

Section 3 - Appendices

INDEX

A

B

INDEX

INDEX

INDEX

INDEX

N

O

P

INDEX

INDEX

INDEX

T

V

W

Z

REFERENCES

ACEP - Bump *Sports Psychology Study Guide*. Human Kinetics, 1989
Alderman R.B. *A Sociological / Psychological Assessment of Attitude toward Physical Activity in Champion Athletes.* Research Quarterly, 41, 1970
* **Backley S.** *The Winning Mind.* Aurum Press, 1996
Beashel P. *Advanced Studies in PE and Sport.* Nelson Thornes, 1996
Biddle S. *European Perspectives on Exercise and Sport Psychology.* Human Kinetics, 1995
Biddle S. *Psychology of Physical Education and Sport - A Practical Guide for Teachers.* FIT systems, 1996
Bull S. *Sport Psychology.* Crowood Press, 1997
Bull S. *The Mental Game Plan, Getting Psyched for Sport.* Sports Dynamics, 1996
* **Bunker L.K. et al.** *Sport Psychology.* Movement Publications, 1985
* **Carron A.V.** *Group Dynamics In Sport.* Spodym Publishers 1988
* **Carron A.V.** *Social Psychology of Sport.* Movement Publications, 1980
* **Carron A.V.** *Social Psychology of Sport: An Experimental Approach.* Movement Publications, 1981
Cattell R.E. and Eber H.W. *Handbook for the 16 P.F. Questionnaire.* IPAT - Champaign Illinois, 1964
Chelladurai P. & Carron A.V. *Leadership.* Canadian Association for PE & Recreation, Ottowa 1978
* **Christina R.W.** *Coaches' Guide to Teaching Sports Skills.* Human Kinetics, 1988
Corbin C. *The Motivational Rating Scale.* Medicine and Science in Sport 9, 1978
Cox R.H. *Sports Psychology Concepts and Applications 4e.* Mosby, 1999
* **Cratty B.J.** *Psychological Preparation and Athletic Performance.* Movement Publications, 1984
* **Cratty B.J.** *Social Psychology of Sport.* Movement Publications, 1980
* **Davies D.** *Psychological Factors in Competitive Sport.* Falmer Press, 1989
Davis R.J. et al *Physical Education and the Study of Sport 4e.* Mosby, 2000
Eysenck H. *Manual for the Eysenck Personality Inventory.* Educational and Industrial Training Service, 1968
Fiedler F. A *Theory of Leadership Effectiveness.* McGraw Hill, 1967
Fisher A.C. *Psychology of Sport.* Merryfield, 1978
Galligan F. et al. *Advanced PE for Edexcel.* Heinemann, 2000
Gill D.L. *Psychological Dynamics of Sport 2e.* Human Kinetics 2000
Gould D. (Weinberg) *Study Guide to Foundations for Sport and Exercise Psychology 2e.* Human Kinetics, 2000
Honeybourne J. *Advanced Physical Education And Sport 2e.* Nelson Thornes, 2000
Honeybourne J. *Advanced Physical Education And Sport 2e Teacher Resource Pack.* Nelson Thornes, 2001
Honeybourne J. *Advanced Physical Education And Sport for AS Level.* Nelson Thornes, 2000
Kenyon G.S. *Six Scales for Assessing Attitude Towards Physical Activity.* Research Quarterly 39, 1968
* **Klavora P. and Daniel J.V.** *Coach, Athlete and Sport Psychologist.* Human Kinetics, 1979
* **Knapp B.** *Skill In Sport.* Routledge and Kegan Paul, 1977
Levleva L. *Inner Sports - Mental Skills for Peak Performance - Audio Edition.* Human Kinetics, 1997
Likert R.A. *A Technique for the Measurement of Attitudes.* Archives of Psychology, 140, 1932
Mace, R. et al. *CD ROM Switch on to Skill in Sport.* Sport in Mind, 2001
Mace, R. et al. *CD ROM Switch on to Sports Psychology.* Sport in Mind, 1999

REFERENCES

Magill R.A. *Motor Learning: Concepts and Applications 6e.* McGraw-Hill, 2000
* **Martens R.** *Social Psychology and Physical Activity.* Murray, 1975
Martens R. *Coaches Guide to Sport Psychology.* Human Kinetics, 1987
Martens R. *Competitive Anxiety in Sport.* Human Kinetics, 1990
Martens R. *Sport Competitive Anxiety Test.* Human Kinetics, 1977
Miller B. *Gold Minds, The Psychology of Winning in Sport.* Crowood Press, 1997
Morris T. *Theories Applications and Issues in Sport Psychology.* Wiley, 1995
* **Mosston M. and Ashworth S.** *Teaching Physical Education.* Merrill, 1986
National Coaching Foundation (NCF). *Psychology and Performance.* NCF 1996
Orlick T. *In Pursuit of Excellence - How to Win in Sport and Life through Mental Training - Audio Edition.* Human Kinetics, 1997
Osgood C. *Semantic Differential Technique: A Sourcebook.* Jam, 1976
Queensland Dept of Education. *Video 5 - Motor Skill Acquisition.* Boulton Hawker, 1988
Roberts G.C. *Learning Experiences in Sports Psychology 2e.* Human Kinetics, 1999
Roberts G.C. *Motivation in Sport and Exercise Science.* Human Kinetics, 1992
Roscoe D. *Skill Acquisition and Sport Psychology - A Teacher's Guide and Answers to Part 2 of Physical Education and the Study of Sport 4e.* Jan Roscoe Publications, 2001
Roscoe D. *OHPs on CDROM, Scientific Elements of AQA / Edexcel / OCR syllabuses.* Jan Roscoe Publications, 2001
Roscoe D. et al. *Physical Education and Sport Studies Advanced Level Student Revision Guide 2e.* Jan Roscoe Publications, 2000
Schmidt R.A. *Motor Learning And Performance 2e.* Human Kinetics, 2000
Schmidt R.A and Lee T.D. *Motor Control and Learning 3e.* Human Kinetics, 1999
Sharp R. *Acquiring Skill in Sport.* Sport Dynamics, 1992
* **Silva J.M. et al.** *Psychological Foundations of Sport.* Human Kinetics, 1984
* **Singer R.N.** *The Learning of Motor Skills.* MacMillan, 1982
* **Singer R.N.** *Motor Learning and Human Performance.* MacMillan, 1982
Speilberger C. *Stress and Anxiety.* Hemisphere, 1977
* **Stallings L.M.** *Motor Learning from Theory To Practice.* Mosby, 1982
Thurston L.L. *Attitudes can be Measured.* American Journal of Sociology, 33, 1928
Vealey R.S. *Conceptualisation of Sport Confidence and Competitive Orientation.* Journal of Sport Psychology Vol 8 pp221-246, 1986
Video Education Australasia. *VideoFit2 - The Learning of Skills - Analysing Physical Activity.* Boulton Hawker, 1996
Weinberg R.S. *Foundations of Sport and Exercise Psychology 2e.* Human Kinetics, 1999
Wesson K. et al. *Sport and PE - A Complete Guide to A Level Study 2e.* Hodder and Stoughton, 2000
* **Willis J.D.** *Exercise Psychology.* Human Kinetics, 1992
Wood B. *Applying Psychology to Sport.* Hodder and Stoughton, 1998

* denotes book out of print at January 2002 - the books however may be found in libraries.

** denotes academic reference, original articles may be found in University libraries.